The
Ridgeway,

National Trail Companion

CW00687422

8th edition published February 2014

© National Trails Office

ISBN 978-0-9561074-5-9

Edited by Martin Fry & Elaine Townson

Photos on pages: 6, 7, 13, 48 (bottom), 53, 60, 61, 62 (top), 66
© Tina Stallard/Natural England

Photos on pages: 11, 18, 23, 47, 48 (top), 56, 59, 62 (bottom), 69, 78, 95 (top)
© Jos Joslin

Photos on pages: 14, 31, 92
© Elaine Townson, National Trails

Photos on pages: 19, 84 (bottom), 95 (bottom)
© Jo Casey, Sunflower Studio

Photos on pages: 29, 84 (top), 93, 94 © Steven Tabbitt

Photo on page: 41 © National Trails

Photo on page: 72 © Ed Hamilton

Photo on page: 83 © Chilterns Conservation Board

Photo on page: 89 © Pete Blyth

Published by

National Trails Office

Signal Court

Old Station Way

Eynsham

OX29 4TL

tel 01865 810224

email nationaltrails@oxfordshire.gov.uk

website www.nationaltrail.co.uk/ridgeway

Designed by Linda Francis
tel 01865 407626

Cover photo:

Ridgeway landscape near Devil's Punchbowl
© Jos Joslin

Contents

Introduction

87 miles (139km) long, much of it following the ancient chalk ridge route used by prehistoric man and surrounded by numerous historic monuments, The Ridgeway offers the chance to get away from the bustle of life in this busy part of England. Perfect, but not too strenuous, for long distance use, this Trail is also ideal for day trips or less. The whole of The Ridgeway can be enjoyed by walkers with horseriders and cyclists able to use all of the western half as far as the River Thames at Streatley and short sections further east.

The Ridgeway

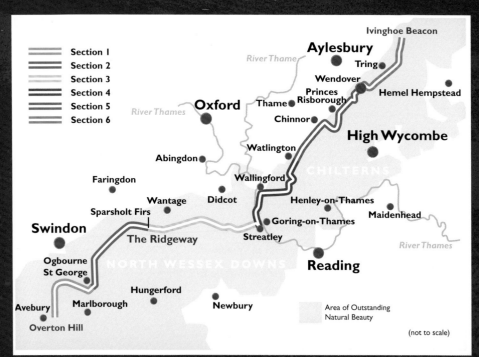

This guide gives you all the information you need to plan an enjoyable visit to The Ridgeway. It has details about accommodation, refreshments, shops, transport, toilets and many other facilities along this National Trail.

The Companion is not a route guide; for detailed information about the Trail itself, The Ridgeway National Trail Guide by Anthony Burton (Aurum Press, 2013) is available from most book shops or online. Alternatively it can be mail ordered from the National Trails Office (see page 16 for details). The Companion complements the Trail Guide and, armed with a copy of each, it is hoped that anyone using The Ridgeway needn't require anything more. Enjoy your trip.

One of only 15 National Trails in England and Wales, The Ridgeway starts in the famous World Heritage Site of Avebury in Wiltshire. It travels for 87 miles (139km) steadily north east along the surprisingly remote scarp ridge of the North Wessex Downs, across the River Thames, and through the Chiltern Hills to finish in the Iron Age fort on top of Ivinghoe Beacon in Buckinghamshire.

The western half of The Ridgeway, as far as Streatley, can be enjoyed by walkers, horseriders and cyclists, whereas only walkers can use the full extent of the eastern half. Despite its relative remoteness, public transport to The Ridgeway is pretty good, especially to the eastern half, where there are several railway stations close to the Trail and an excellent bus network. With a little planning many places along the western half can also be reached by bus or train or a combination of the two.

The Ridgeway passes through two distinctive protected landscapes, both designated Areas of Outstanding Natural Beauty (AONB). The western half of the Trail travels through the open expansive downland of the North Wessex Downs AONB, whilst east of the Thames it stays amongst the more gentle and wooded countryside of the Chilterns AONB.

In the west The Ridgeway travels as a broad ancient track along the open and fairly isolated top of the chalk downland ridge, often several kilometres from the nearest village. Here, to the south is rolling downland and to the north, at the bottom of the steep scarp slope, the wide expanse of the Thames Valley. The far-reaching views are

I INTRODUCTION

dominated by the sky, the clouds and small clumps of beech woodland and all you may have for company is a solitary skylark singing overhead or a hare chasing across an adjacent field.

In the past these downs were sheep grazed, but since the introduction of fertilisers in the first half of the last century many areas have been ploughed and planted with crops. However sheep grazing does continue in places and, in others, a characteristic sight is immaculately managed grass tracks, the gallops used for training racehorses. The excellent turf of the downs makes this prime horse country but you need to be up early to see the strings of racehorses exercising.

At Streatley The Ridgeway crosses the River Thames and another of England's National Trails, the Thames Path, and enters more intimate and less open countryside. It follows the bank of the River Thames along a lovely 5 miles (8km) rural stretch before heading eastwards into the Chiltern Hills. Mostly on narrower paths, the Trail passes through woodlands, many of them beech, over neatly cultivated fields and across chalk grassland nature reserves rich in wildflowers. In contrast to the western half, although its usually peaceful here, you're never far from pleasant small towns or attractive villages.

With the support of Natural England, The Ridgeway is managed to the highest standards necessary for one of the most important paths in the country by the local highway authorities with a small dedicated team of staff and local volunteers.

Sheep on Pitstone Hill, Buckinghamshire

For thousands of years, at least 5,000 and maybe many more, people have walked or ridden The Ridgeway, be they drovers, traders, invaders or today's recreational visitors. As part of a prehistoric track once stretching about 250 miles (400km) from the Dorset coast to the Wash on the Norfolk coast, The Ridgeway provided a route over the high ground for travellers which was less wooded and drier than routes through the springline villages below.

New Stone Age men, the first farmers in Britain, left the earliest remains. Their long barrows can be found at a few places both west and east of the River Thames. It was Bronze Age people from later times, around 2,000 BC, however, who dragged the huge sarsen stones from the surrounding hills and formed the dramatic Avebury Circle. There are many of their round burial barrows along the length of the National Trail.

Hill forts built during the Iron Age from about 500 BC until the Romans arrived in 43 AD are also found both sides of the Thames. These forts command the high ground and in several places they defended The Ridgeway against attack from the north.

In the Dark Ages The Ridgeway was a main route for the Saxons and Vikings who fought many battles during their advances into Wessex. In medieval times it was drovers driving livestock from Wales and the West Country to the Home Counties, not armies, who used The Ridgeway.

Until the Enclosure Acts of 1750 The Ridgeway was a broad band of tracks along the crest of the downs where travellers chose the driest or most convenient path. During Enclosures the exact course and width of The Ridgeway was defined by the building of earth banks and the planting of thorn hedges to prevent livestock straying into the newly cultivated fields.

In recent times use of The Ridgeway has changed greatly; farmers do still use much of it as an access route to their fields for tractors and other machinery but its main use is no longer utilitarian but recreational with walkers and riders out for exercise, pleasure and spiritual refreshment.

Avebury stones

III WILDLIFE

The grasslands which occur on the chalk of the downs and the Chilterns are some of the most interesting habitats in England and some of the richest in terms of the number of plant species found. Chalk grassland has suffered from modern farming and much has disappeared under the plough. However those unimproved chalk grassland areas along The Ridgeway, especially the nature reserves east of the Thames, are well worth visiting where you'll find, amongst many other lovely plants, several types of orchid.

Another botanical treat in store for visitors during springtime is the carpet of bluebells in many of the woodlands in the Chilterns, usually in the first couple of weeks of May.

For those keen on seeing birds, The Ridgeway should not disappoint you. A range of relatively common birds such as warblers and finches are found the length of The Ridgeway enjoying the food supply provided by the hedges lining the Trail. Skylarks, yellowhammers and corn buntings are particularly characteristic of the downland and although generally in decline in Britain are still fairly numerous along The Ridgeway. The song of the corn bunting, likened to the sound of a jangle of keys, is the distinctive sound of the western half of The Ridgeway.

In colder months flocks of redwings and fieldfares, winter visitors from Scandinavia, are common and are usually seen feeding in the fields surrounding the Trail. However, most people will especially cherish the site of a red kite and you'll be unlucky if you don't see one in the Chiltern Hills and increasingly west of the Thames too. These magnificent birds of prey recognised by their forked tail were reintroduced to this area in the late 1980s and are now well established. In woodlands of this area too, woodpeckers and nuthatches may well be spotted.

Apart from the ubiquitous rabbit, hares and deer are the larger wild animals you may encounter. Hares are found in open countryside and are bigger than rabbits with longer ears and hind legs. They are solitary animals and most active at night, so late evening or early morning are the best times to see them. Two species of deer are found on The Ridgeway, roe and fallow with the former being the smaller and also living in smaller groups of just three or four animals. Both of these species are nocturnal and shy so, as for hares, being on The Ridgeway at dusk or dawn will give you the best chance of viewing them.

Walkers

Walkers can use the whole length of the Trail. There are also a series of circular walks available that use sections of The Ridgeway - details on The Ridgeway website.

Cyclists and Horseriders

Riders, both cyclists and horseriders, can share The Ridgeway with walkers all the way from the start at Overton Hill near Avebury to Streatley on the River Thames, a distance of roughly 43 miles (68km). Once across the river the only long section of the Trail which can be ridden is the 8-miles (13-km) stretch which follows the Icknield Way through the Chilterns from Britwell Hill near Watlington to Wainhill on the Oxfordshire/Buckinghamshire border. In other places The Ridgeway is a footpath and it is a trespass offence to ride on a footpath without the permission of the landowner.

However an alternative for riders is to join the Swan's Way long distance bridleway at Goring-on-Thames, just across the river from Streatley, and to follow this mostly on The Ridgeway to Bledlow west of Princes Risborough (here the Swan's Way turns north). From Bledlow riders can pick up the Icknield Way Riders' Route which provides a good alternative to The Ridgeway for riders as far as Pitstone Hill, just a couple of kilometres from Ivinghoe Beacon. Unfortunately riders can't continue to Ivinghoe Beacon, the official end of the National Trail, since the route to it is on footpaths.

There are some circular rides for cyclists and horseriders that use sections of The Ridgeway - details on The Ridgeway website.

Vehicles

Recreational vehicles can now only use about 20% (17 miles) of The Ridgeway and, apart from two short sections, only from May until the end of September each year.

V PREPARING FOR YOUR VISIT

Deciding where to start

The Ridgeway can be walked in either direction and is signposted both ways. The route is generally promoted from west to east, starting at Overton Hill and finishing on Ivinghoe Beacon, because prevailing winds tend to come from the southwest and so will be behind you.

How far to walk in a day

How far you walk in a day is obviously up to you and will depend on your fitness and experience. As a guide, people generally walk at about 2½ miles (4km) an hour but on sections with climbs and descents slightly longer should be allowed. If you are planning to walk the whole length of The Ridgeway, or for several days, it is usually sensible to plan a short first day to ease yourself in gently.

What to take with you

- Carry warm and waterproof clothing as even on some summer days wind and rain can make a walk or ride uncomfortable.

- Walkers should wear strong, comfortable footwear. During the summer trainers are usually OK for a walk on The Ridgeway, but during wet periods and winter months wear walking boots or even Wellingtons if you're comfortable walking in these. Take a blister repair kit, just in case.

- Wear protection (hat and lotion) against the sun during the summer – the western half of the Trail is particularly exposed.

- Carry water if walking or riding for more than a couple of hours – water points west of the River Thames are relatively infrequent.

- If your walk or ride is along unfamiliar paths don't forget your map and/or guidebook!

Personal safety

If you are walking/riding alone it's sensible, as a simple precaution, to let someone know where you are and when you expect to arrive/return. Do bear in mind that mobile phone coverage can be patchy in rural areas, so you cannot always rely on it.

Dog Matters

If you are planning to undertake a long distance walk along The Ridgeway with your dog, you are advised to ensure it is fit before you start; on occasions walkers have had to abandon a walk because their dogs can't keep up! There are wax products available for applying to dogs' pads to help prevent soreness ... they might be worth investigating.

Please also make sure your dog is under close control at all times to prevent it from disturbing livestock or wildlife. You are asked to keep your dog on a lead when you're in the few fields you'll encounter with livestock, although if you find that cattle seriously harass you because of the dog, it's wise to let it off the lead.

VI HOW TO FOLLOW THE TRAIL

The Official National Trail Guide

The Ridgeway National Trail Guide by Anthony Burton, Aurum Press 2013. The official guide to the Trail with written route descriptions and colour 1:25,000 Ordnance Survey maps. Cost £12.99. *Available from the National Trails Office, see page 16.*

Maps

It's usually a good idea to use maps when walking, particularly in unfamiliar areas. The official National Trail Guide includes colour sections of all the appropriate 1:25 000 Ordnance Survey maps needed to follow The Ridgeway. Alternatively, to enjoy and interpret the wider landscape, you can purchase your own Ordnance Survey maps.

The Landranger series (pink cover at 1:50 000 or 2cm to 1km) has all public rights of way, viewpoints, tourist information and selected places of interest marked on them. For the whole of The Ridgeway you will need:

173 Swindon and Devizes
174 Newbury and Wantage
175 Reading and Windsor
165 Aylesbury and Leighton Buzzard

The larger scale Explorer series (orange cover at 1:25 000 or 4cm to 1km) has more detail including fence lines which can be very helpful when following rights of way, recreational routes and greater tourist information. For the whole of The Ridgeway you will need:

157 Marlborough and Savernake Forest
170 Abingdon, Wantage and Vale of White Horse
171 Chiltern Hills West
181 Chiltern Hills North

The Ridgeway A-Z Adventure Atlas. Geographers' A-Z Map Company Ltd, 2013.

Ridgeway* Harvey Maps, 2008 - 1:40 000 scale waterproof map of The Ridgeway including information on a range of facilities along the Trail. *Available from the National Trails Office, see page 16.*

Signage

The Ridgeway follows a series of well-signed public rights of way and minor roads (91% of the Trail is off road).

The acorn is the symbol of National Trails and is used on all The Ridgeway signage.

In most cases the signs, or waymark discs on gates or posts, will also carry the word 'Ridgeway'. The status of the right of way, which defines who can use it, will also be shown either in words, or by using the national waymarking scheme of coloured arrows – see below:

Footpath

Bridleway

Restricted Byway

Byway

The downs near Wantage

13

VII PUBLICATIONS

Other Guides and Publications about The Ridgeway

Available from National Trails Office, see page 16

The Ridgeway National Trail Guide* by Anthony Burton, Aurum Press 2013 - the official guide with written route descriptions from Overton Hill to Ivinghoe Beacon and colour 1:25 000 maps.

The Ridgeway National Trail by Steve Davison, Cicerone Guide 2013.

The Ridgeway: Avebury to Ivinghoe Beacon by Nick Hill, Trailblazer Publications, 2012.

Walking in Britain, Lonely Planet, 2007 - includes a description of the western half of The Ridgeway.

The Greater Ridgeway by Ray Quinlan, Cicerone, 2003. Describes a route from Lyme Regis to Hunstanton, including The Ridgeway National Trail.

Exploring the Ridgeway by Alan Charles, Countryside Books 2000 - based on 14 circular walks covering The Ridgeway from Ivinghoe Beacon to Overton Hill.

The Oldest Road - an Exploration of the Ridgeway by J R L Anderson with photographs by Fay Godwin. Paperback edition by Whittet Books, 1992.

Let's Hear it for The Ridgeway!* by Elizabeth Newbery - a family activity book full of ideas and information on things to do and see on and close to The Ridgeway.

Cycling towards Monkton Down

The following companies offer self-guided or guided holiday packages on part or all of The Ridgeway.

Walking

Celtic Trails Walking Holidays **T**: 01291 689774 www.celtic-trails.com

Contours Walking Holidays **T**: 01629 821900 www.contours.co.uk

Discovery Travel **T:** 01904 632226 www.discoverytravel.co.uk

Explore Britain **T**: 01740 650900 www.explorebritain.com

Freedom Walking Holidays www.freedomwalkingholidays.co.uk

Macs Adventure **T**: 0141 530 8120 www.macsadventure.com

Ridgeway Walks **T:** 01491 200423 www.ridgewaywalks.com

Walk The Landscape **T:** 07718 660070 www.walkthelandscape.co.uk

Baggage Transfer

Carrier Bags **T:** 07733 885390 **E:** anthonyewen@hotmail.co.uk
www.ridgewaytransportation.co.uk

Accommodation Providers Many will transport your luggage to your next night's accommodation.

Cycling

History on Your Handlebars **T**: 01249 730013 www.historyonyourhandlebars. co.uk - weekend or day tour including part of The Ridgeway.

Horse Riding

Pewsey Vale Riding Centre, Church Farm, Stanton St Bernard, Marlborough SN8 4LJ **T**: 01672 851400 - www.pewseyvaleridingcentre.com

IX USEFUL CONTACTS

The Ridgeway National Trails Office

National Trails Office, Signal Court, Old Station Way, Eynsham OX29 4TL. **T**: 01865 810224. **E:** nationaltrails@oxfordshire.gov.uk

Highway Authorities responsible for public rights of way

Buckinghamshire County Council **T**: 0845 370 8090 www.buckscc.gov.uk

Hertfordshire County Council **T**: 0300 123 4040 www.hertsdirect.org

Oxfordshire County Council **T**: 01865 810226 www.oxfordshire.gov.uk

Swindon Borough Council **T**: 01793 445500 www.swindon.gov.uk

West Berkshire Council **T**: 01635 42400 www.westberks.gov.uk

Wiltshire Council **T**: 0300 456 0100 www.wiltshire.gov.uk

Agency responsible for National Trails

Natural England **T**: 0845 6003078 www.naturalengland.org.uk

Areas of Outstanding Natural Beauty

North Wessex Downs AONB **T**: 01488 685440 www.northwessexdowns.org.uk

Chilterns AONB **T**: 01844 355500 www.chilternsaonb.org

Organisations for walkers

Backpackers Club - www.backpackersclub.co.uk

Long Distance Walkers Association - www.ldwa.org.uk

Oxford Fieldpaths Society - www.ofs.org.uk

Ramblers Association **T**: 020 7339 8500 www.ramblers.org.uk

Organisations for cyclists

British Cycling Federation **T**: 0161 274 2000 www.britishcycling.org.uk

Cyclists Touring Club (Off-Road) **T**: 01483 238337 www.ctc.org.uk

Sustrans **T**: 0117 9268893 www.sustrans.org.uk

The Rough Stuff Fellowship www.rsf.org.uk

Organisations for horseriders

British Horse Society **T**: 02476 840500 www.bhs.org.uk

Byways & Bridleways Trust - www.bbtrust.org.uk

Endurance GB **T**: 02476 697929 www.endurancegb.co.uk

Tourist Information providers

Details of these are included in the introductory pages to each of the six sections of The Ridgeway.

Other organisations

Berkshire, Buckinghamshire & Oxfordshire Wildlife Trust **T**: 01865 775476 www.bbowt.org.uk

Chiltern Society **T**: 01494 771250 www.chilternsociety.org.uk

Friends of the Ridgeway - www.ridgewayfriends.org.uk

Herts & Middlesex Wildlife Trust **T**: 01727 858901 www.hertswildlifetrust.org.uk

Wiltshire Wildlife Trust **T**: 01380 725670 www.wiltshirewildlife.org

X GETTING THERE

Getting to The Ridgeway by public transport is fairly easy, particularly the eastern half of the Trail. Visit our website www.nationaltrail.co.uk/ridgeway to find a map-based online travel planner with information on train and bus services.

Alternatively, telephone numbers and websites to find out more about public transport to the Trail are listed below:

- Rail Services   08457 484950 (24 hours a day)
        www.nationalrail.co.uk

- Bus Services   0871 2002233
        www.traveline.info

- Taxi Services   Information is included in each of the six sections

We encourage people to consider using public transport rather than travelling by private car as this is better for the environment, helps to support local public transport services and reduces congestion from parking in the smaller settlements. However, those wishing to travel to The Ridgeway by car are asked to park considerately if parking in villages on or close to the Trail. Other places to park are listed within each section.

• Be safe – plan ahead and follow any signs

Even when going out locally, it's best to get the latest information about where and when you can go. Follow advice and local signs, and be prepared for the unexpected.

• Leave gates and property as you find them

Please respect the working life of the countryside, as our actions can affect people's livelihoods, our heritage, and the safety and welfare of animals and ourselves.

• Protect plants and animals, and take your litter home

We have a responsibility to protect our countryside now and for future generations, so make sure you don't harm animals, birds, plants or trees.

• Keep your dog under close control

The countryside is a great place to exercise dogs, but it's every owner's duty to make sure their dog is not a danger or nuisance to farm animals, wildlife or other people.

• Consider other people

Showing consideration and respect for other people makes the countryside a pleasant environment for everyone – at home, at work and at leisure.

For further details visit www.countrysideaccess.gov.uk

Red kite

XII EMERGENCY CONTACTS

We hope you will not need to refer to this page during your visit but the information below will help you find the service you need quickly should something unforeseen occur. In urgent and life threatening situations, or when a crime is in progress, the emergency services can be contacted on **999 or 112**.

When the situation is not an emergency please use the following contact details:

Police

To contact local police stations dial 101

Hospitals

The following hospitals with casualty departments are located in the places shown below. The telephone numbers given are the hospital switchboard; ask to be put through to Accident and Emergency Reception.

◆ Full 24-hour emergency service

▲ Minor injuries only (MIU), NOT 24-hour service

Section	Town	Telephone No	Address
1&2	◆ Swindon	01793 604020	The Great Western Hospital, Marlborough Road, Swindon SN3 6BB
3&4	▲ Abingdon	01235 205700	Abingdon Community Hospital, Marcham Road, Abingdon OX14 1AG
3&4	◆ Oxford	01865 741166	John Radcliffe Hospital Headley Way, Headington Oxford OX3 9DU
3&4	▲ Wallingford	01491 208500	Wallingford Community Hospital, Reading Road, Wallingford OX10 9DU (Mon-Fri 8:30-18:30)
5&6	◆ Aylesbury	01296 315000	Stoke Mandeville Hospital, Mandeville Road, Aylesbury HP21 8AL

ACCOMMODATION, FACILITIES & SERVICES XIII

The following chapters give details of the settlements, accommodation, eating places, shops, attractions and other facilities along or near The Ridgeway. They are listed in geographic order from Overton Hill to Ivinghoe Beacon.

If you fail to find accommodation using this guide please contact the Visitor Information Centre listed near the beginning of each section which may be able to provide other addresses.

To find map grid references for individual accommodation put postcodes into www.nearby.org.uk

You are strongly advised to book accommodation in advance. Whilst booking, do check prices since those quoted here are usually the minimum charged. It's also wise to book evening meals in advance if eating in village pubs as they can get very busy.

For those who would like to enjoy more than a day on The Ridgeway without having to carry all their possessions, many accommodation providers have indicated whether they are willing to transport the luggage you don't need during the day to your next night's accommodation. The fee charged for this service needs to be discussed and agreed at the time of the booking. Accommodation providers have also indicated if they are willing to collect you from The Ridgeway and deliver you back after your stay.

All the information within this Companion is as accurate as possible. Inclusion of accommodation does not constitute a recommendation although it is indicated in the details whether an establishment has a recognised grade awarded to it. If you have any comments or notice any errors, please write to the National Trails Office (page 16).

Camping on The Ridgeway

The situation regarding camping on The Ridgeway is, in theory, clear enough; The Ridgeway is privately owned and the public right of way along it is for passage only, not for stopping and camping.

In practice, however, most landowners do not object if a tent is pitched on The Ridgeway for a night and disappears the next morning as long as no litter is left, no damage done, nor camp fires lit. Do not camp in adjoining fields, woods or gallops without prior permission from the landowner.

XIII ACCOMMODATION, FACILITIES & SERVICES

Key to Symbols for Settlements

Any comments relate to preceding icon

⊕   map grid reference (see start of each section for relevant maps)

👢   shortest walking distance from The Ridgeway

🚆   most convenient train station

P£   car park (paying)

P F   car park (free)

⊕   toilets

&.WC   toilets adapted for disabled users

ℹ️   Visitor Information Centre

🍺   pub (usually open lunchtimes 11:00-15:00 then evenings 18:00-23:00). Names and telephone numbers of pubs are given for those settlements with up to two pubs

✗   bar meals in pub

✉️   post office (usual opening hours 09:00-17:30 weekdays; 09:00-12:30 Sat)

🛒   general store (usual opening hours daily 09:00-17:30 Mon-Sat)

☕   cafe/tea shop

🍽️   restaurant

🥡   food take-away

▯▯▯▯▯▯▯▯▯▯▯   opening hours of services relate to the preceding symbol
S M T W T F S

eg: ▯ open all day   ▮ closed all day

      ▯ Post offices, general stores,   ▯ Post offices, general stores,
        cafe/tea shops - open morning;   cafe/tea shops - open afternoon;
        Pubs, bar meals, restaurants,   Pubs, bar meals, restaurants,
        takeaways - open lunchtime   takeaways - open evening

£   bank (usually open daily 9.30am-4.30pm Mon-Fri)

▣   cash machine available, including outside bank opening hours

☆   tourist attraction

Key to Symbols for Accommodation

Type of accommodation (symbols in margins)

▲ hostel

Ⅹ camping

[H] hotel

[INN] inn

B&B bed and breakfast

♄ horse accommodation

SC self catering

The Plough, Lower Cadsden

XIII ACCOMMODATION, FACILITIES & SERVICES

The number and price following the symbols for rooms gives the number and price of that type of room available. The same applies to tent/caravan pitches and stabling/grazing for horses. Prices quoted for rooms are the minimum price per room per night for bed and breakfast. The price for single occupancy of a double or twin room is given in brackets eg (£35.00).

Accommodation symbols - hotels, inns, guest houses, B&Bs and hostels

🛏	double room	⒢	grazing for horses
🛏	twin room	⒮	stabling for horses
🛏	family room	🚲	secure cycle storage
🛏	single room	DRY	clothes/boots drying facilities
👫	children welcome	▣	laundry facilities
♿	wheelchair access	🚗	transport to and from Trail by arrangement
🐕	dogs allowed by arrangement		
V	caters for vegetarians	🚶	luggage transported to next overnight stop by arrangement
●	most food locally produced		
●	some food locally produced	📶	free Wifi
●	most food is organic	VISA	credit card(s) accepted
○	some food is organic	★	VisitEngland accommodation standard
🎒	packed lunches available		
⦿	evening meals available by arrangement	⛴	special feature/comment

Accommodation symbols - camping and caravan sites

⛺	tent pitches	▣	showers
🚐	caravan pitches	🚲	secure cycle storage
🚰	cold water	▣	laundry facilities
🚰	hot water	🏪	site shop
🚻	toilets	CG	camping gas
♿WC	toilets adapted for disabled users	⛴	special feature/comment

Section 1

Overton Hill to Ogbourne St George

Starting in the Avebury World Heritage Site with its wealth
of archaeology, this 9.3 miles (14.8km) stretch of The Ridgeway
climbs gradually to a high point at Barbury Castle Iron Age fort.
From there the route along Smeathe's Ridge provides great views
on either side as it gently descends to the valley of the River Og.

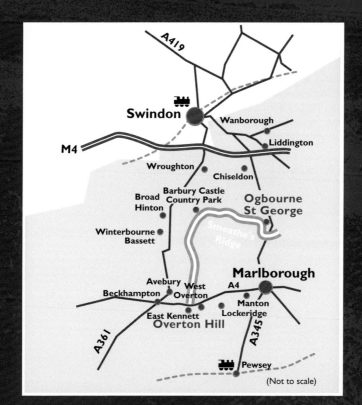

(Not to scale)

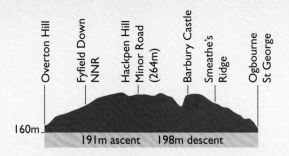

160m — 191m ascent · 198m descent

Overton Hill · Fyfield Down NNR · Hackpen Hill Minor Road (264m) · Barbury Castle · Smeathe's Ridge · Ogbourne St George

Maps

| Landranger maps | 173 | Swindon and Devizes |
| Explorer maps | 157 | Marlborough and Savernake Forest |

Taxis

Place	Name	Telephone Number
Marlborough	Arrow Private Hire	01672 515567
	Kayze Cars	01672 514556
	Marlborough Taxis	01672 512786
	Paddy's Taxis	01672 511884

Car Parking

If you choose to park in villages close to The Ridgeway, please park considerately. Other places to park are listed below but you need to be aware that theft from cars parked in the countryside does occur. You are advised to leave any unnecessary items at home or, failing that, ensure that anything valuable is locked in the boot of your vehicle.

Place	Map Grid Reference
On Ridgeway at the start at Overton Hill, on north side of A4, 4 1/2 miles (7km) west of Marlborough	SU 119681
On Ridgeway at Hackpen Hill on minor road between Marlborough and Broad Hinton, 2 miles (3km) south east of Broad Hinton	SU 129747
On Ridgeway at Barbury Castle Country Park, 5 miles (8km) south of Swindon signed from Wroughton and Chiseldon	SU 157760

Water Points

Place	Map Grid Reference
Elm Tree Cottage, Southend (please ask before using)	SU 198734

Toilets

Place	Map Grid Reference
Barbury Castle Country Park	SU 155762

Vets

Place	Name	Telephone Number
Marlborough	The Drove Veterinary Hospital	01672 512043
	Riverside Veterinary Centre	01672 514875

Farriers

Place	Name	Telephone Number
Marlborough	J Baker	01672 514013
	AP Marshall	01672 562670
	ND Quinlan	07912 566780
	AJ Turnell	07768 535271
Aldbourne	Peter Baker	01672 540812
Wroughton	P A Groom	01793 814185

Saddlers

Place	Name	Telephone Number
Marlborough	G & S Saddlery	01672 569288
Tockenham, Swindon	Old Dairy Saddlery	01793 849284

Riding Stables for Guided Rides

Place	Name	Telephone Number
Chiseldon	Ladysmith Equestrian Centre	01793 740439

Horsebox Parking

The following places have sufficient space for you to park your horsebox. You **must** call in advance to arrange as space may be scarce. A fee may also be charged.

Place	Name	Telephone Number
Marlborough	Brown's Farm (Accommodation guests and day-riders)	01672 515129
Ogbourne St George	Foxlynch (Accommodation guests and day-riders)	01672 841307

Bike Repairs

Place	Name	Telephone Number
Marlborough	Acceler8 Cycles	01672 513414
	Bertie Maffoons	01672 519119
	Fix the Bike	07785 926021
Swindon	Bike Doctor	01793 874873
	Dans Cycles	01793 423380
	Hargroves Cycles	01793 528208
	Mitchell Cycles	01793 523306
	Swindon Cycles Superstore	01793 700105
	Total Bike	01793 644185

Mountain Bike Hire

Place	Name	Telephone Number
Marlborough	Bertie Maffoons	01672 519119
	Fix the Bike	07785 926021
Swindon	Swindon Cycles Superstore	01793 700105

Visitor Information Centres

These VICs are staffed but note that many libraries in the area also have leaflets about local attractions and events.

★ offers accommodation booking service

Place
★ Swindon

Address/Opening Hours
Central Library, Regents Circus, Swindon SN1 1QG
T: 01793 466454
E: infocentre@swindon.gov.uk
www.visitwiltshire.co.uk/swindon
Opening hours:
All year: Mon-Fri 09:30-17:00
Sat 09:30-16:00

Hoar frost at Upham

Browns Farm

Marlborough, Wilts
Tel 01672 515129

Peaceful farmhouse set on the edge of Savernake Forest.
B&B accommodation: Tea/coffee facilities, some with en-suite facilities.
TV Lounge and large gardens available for guests. Free Wifi in B&B

Also 3 self contained
properties for
self catering.

Ideal base for touring Wiltshire. Immediate access to footpaths &
bridleways. Stables and fields available for horses.
Working Beef/Arable Farm. Ample off-street parking.

MARLBOROUGH

⌖ **SU1969** 👟 **4.4 miles (7km)**
🚂 **Pusey 6.9 miles (11.1 km)** 🎒

Town with full range of services. Visit www.marlboroughwiltshire.co.uk for further details, including information about a range of accommodation.

B&B ☺ **Browns Farm**
SC

⌖ GR SU198678 0.9miles(1.5km) south of Marlborough
Mrs Hazel J Crockford
Browns Farm, Marlborough SN8 4ND
T: 01672 515129 **M:** 07931 311985
E: crockford@farming.co.uk
www. marlboroughholidaycottages.com
🛏 1 £50 🛏 1 £45 (£30) 🛏 1 £65
⚥ 📺 V 🍴 ⚘ 🚲 **DRY** 🚗 👣 💳
Most major cards. Some rooms en-suite
Ⓢ 2 £10 Ⓖ 4 £10
🎒 Free WiFi in B&B. 3 self contained properties for self-catering also available from £200/week ★★★ Horsebox parking available for day-riders

Sarsen stone (detail)

Postern Hill Campsite ⛺

Ian St Clair
Postern Hill, Marlborough
SN8 4ND
T: 01672 515195 **M:** 07896 628217
E: postern.hill@campingintheforest.co.uk
www. campingintheforest.co.uk
⛺ £12/pitch or 🚐 £23/pitch 📺 🔥
♨ ⓗ 🚲 🏪 CG **VISA** Most major cards ★★★
🎒 170 pitches total. No toilets during winter months

MANTON

⌖ **SU1768** 👟 **4.1 miles (6.6km) avoiding main road**
🚂 **Pewsey 6 miles (9.7km)**

🍺 |‖‖‖‖‖‖‖‖‖| ✕ |‖‖‖‖‖‖‖‖‖|
　　S M T W T F S 　　 S M T W T F S

Pub: Outside Chance 01672 512352

Beech Hill B&B

Mrs Elizabeth Bonham
Manton Drove, Manton, Marlborough
SN8 4HL
T: 01672 519833
E: liz.bonham@virgin.net
www.beechhillhouse.net

🛏/🛏 3 £80 (£50) ⚥V 🍴 ● **DRY** All rooms ensuite

LOCKERIDGE

SU1467 1.6 miles (2.5km)
Pewsey 7.1 miles (11.4km)

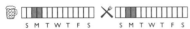

S M T W T F S   S M T W T F S

Pub: Who'd A Thought It Inn 01672 861255

B&B | **Taffrail** | *closed Dec*

Mrs Julia Spencer
Back Lane, Lockeridge, Marlborough
SN8 4ED
T: 01672 861266
E: spencer@taffrail.eclipse.co.uk
www.uktravelandtourism.com

1 £50 2 £50 (£30) (min age 8) V O DRY
No evening meals locally on Mondays

WEST OVERTON

SU1367 0.6 miles (1km)
Pewsey 8.5 miles (13.6km)

S M T W T F S   S M T W T F S

Pub: Bell Inn 01672 861099

EAST KENNETT

SU1267 0.4 miles (0.7km)
Pewsey 11 miles (18km)

Old Forge | **B&B**

Mrs Laura Feeley
East Kennett, Marlborough SN8 4EY
T: 01672 861686 **M:** 07770 871066
E: laura@feeleyfamily.fsnet.co.uk
www.theoldforge-avebury.co.uk
3 £70 (£60) 1 £75 (£60)
1 £105 V O
Visa, Mastercard ★★★★ Some rooms en-suite
VisitEngland Gold Award.

Beckhampton Bed & Breakfast

www.aveburyworld.co.uk
Tel 01672 539534/07919 342103
Email: info@aveburyworld.co.uk

Prices from £40 per night
Seasonal opening - Spring to Autumn

- Within Avebury World Heritage Site
- Free transport to/from The Ridgeway
- Hot Tub
- Cream Teas
- Opposite Waggon & Horses Pub
- Seasonal Offers/ Rambler Specials

BECKHAMPTON

SU0968 1.8 miles (3km)
Swindon 12 miles (19.5km)

S M T W T F S   S M T W T F S

Pub: Waggon and Horses 01672 539418

B&B Beckhampton *closed winter*

Mr and Mrs Hamersley
Isobel Cottage, Beckhampton,
Marlborough SN8 1QJ
T: 01672 539534 **M:** 07919 342103
E: info@aveburyworld.co.uk
www.aveburyworld.co.uk
/ 2 £70 (£55) 1 £40 V
Most major cards

AVEBURY

SU1069 1.2 miles (2km)
Pewsey 10.6 miles (17km) PF
WC

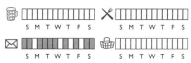

S M T W T F S   S M T W T F S

S M T W T F S   S M T W T F S

S M T W T F S

Pub: Red Lion 01672 539266

☆ Avebury World Heritage Site
T: 01672 539250
www.nationaltrust.org.uk

☆ Alexander Keiller Museum
www.nationaltrust.org.uk

☆ Avebury Manor and Garden
www.nationaltrust.org.uk

Manor Farm *closed Xmas & Easter* **B&B**

Mrs Judith Farthing
High Street, Avebury, Marlborough
SN8 1RF
T: 01672 539294
www.manorfarmavebury.com
1 £90 1 £90 (£70) (min
age 12) V ★★★★
Private bathroom

Aveburylife **B&B**

Mrs Antoinette Kremer
5 Trusloe Cottages, Avebury Trusloe,
Marlborough SN8 1QZ
T: 01672 539644 **M:** 07788 443632
E: antoinette@aveburylife.com
www.aveburylife.com
/ 1 £70 (£45) 1 £40
V O Double room
en-suite

Avebury Lodge *closed 25th & 26th Dec* **B&B**

Mr Andrew Blackall
The Lodge, High Street, Avebury,
Marlborough SN8 1RF
T: 01672 539023
E: avebury@email.com
www.aveburylodge.co.uk
2 £175 (£140) 1£250 V
O Mastercard, Visa.
Some rooms en-suite
This is a vegetarian B&B. WiFi in
rooms

33

WINTERBOURNE BASSETT

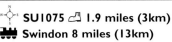 **SU1075** 🛏 1.9 miles (3km)
🚂 Swindon 8 miles (13km)

Pub: White Horse Inn 01793 731257

BROAD HINTON

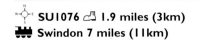 **SU1076** 🛏 1.9 miles (3km)
🚂 Swindon 7 miles (11km)

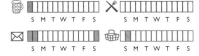

Cashback in Post Office
Pubs: Crown Inn 01793 731302 &
Barbury Inn 01793 731510

WROUGHTON

 **SU1480** 🛏 2.7 miles (4.3km)
🚂 Swindon 3.8 miles (6.1km) PF

Large village with range of services
☆ Wroughton Science Museum (Library
& Archive)
T: 01793 846222
www.sciencemuseum.org.uk/wroughton
Visit by appointment only

Alexandra House   *closed Xmas & New Year* Ⓗ

Raymond McKibben
Wittingham Drive, Wroughton Swindon
SN4 0QJ
T: 01793 819000
E: reception.alexandra@principal-
hayley.com
www.swindonalexandrahouse.co.uk
🛏116 £82 (£72) 🛏20 £82 (£72)
🛏 16 £102 ♛⛷ 🔊 V ● O Ⓢ Ⓘ
All major cards ★★★★ All rooms
en-suite

CHISELDON

 **SU1879** 🛏 1.9 miles (3km)
🚂 Swindon 5 miles (8km) PF

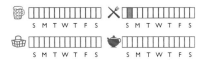

▣ In petrol station/café
Pub: Plough Inn (Badbury) 01793 740342
☆ Chiseldon Museum **T:** 01793 740784
Closed in winter

Courtleigh House   B

Mrs Ruth Hibberd
40 Draycott Road, Chiseldon, Swindon
SN4 0LS
T: 01793 740246 **M:** 07896 296909
E: courtleighhouse@yahoo.co.uk
🛏 1 £90 🛏 1 £90 (£50) ♛ V ● O
&🚲 DRY 🚘 Some rooms en-suite
Ⓗ Lift available to pub for evening meal

B&B Rossendale

Mrs Anne Wirdnam
44a Station Road, Chiseldon, Swindon
SN4 0PW
T: 01793 740726 **M:** 07854 192417
E: anne@rossendale.biz
www.rossendale.biz

🛏 1 £75 (£55) 🛏 1 £70 🛏 1 £95
🛏 1 £45 ⛹ V ● ○ 🚲 **DRY** ◎ 🚗
👣 ★★★★ Some rooms en-suite

Ⓗ Chiseldon House Hotel

Mrs Sue Higgs
New Road, Chiseldon, Swindon
SN4 0NE
T: 01793 741010
E: welcome@chiseldonhouse.com
www.chiseldonhouse.com

🛏 15 £120 🛏 3 £120 (£100) 🛏 1
£140 🛏 1 £100 ⛹ ♿ V ● ○ ⚠ ◐
🚲 **DRY** ◎ 👣 **VISA** Most major cards
★★★ All rooms en-suite

OGBOURNE ST GEORGE

✥ **SU2074** 👣 **0.6 miles (1km)**
🚂 **Swindon 8 miles (13km)**

🍺 ▯▯▯▯▯▯▯▯▯▯ ✕ ▯▯▯▯▯▯▯▯
   S M T W T F S   S M T W T F S

Pubs: Inn with The Well 01672 841445
& Parklands Hotel 01672 84155
Winter opening times vary. Please check

Inn with the Well

Mr Michael Shaw
Marlborough Road, Ogbourne St
George, Marlborough SN8 1SQ
T: 01672 841445
E: info@theinnwiththewell.co.uk
www.theinnwiththewell.co.uk

🛏 3 £70 🛏 2 £70 🛏 1 £90 ⛹
♿ 🔲 V ● ○ ⚠ ◐ 🚲 **DRY** 🚗 👣
VISA Most major cards ★★★ All rooms
en-suite
▌ No evening meals Sundays October
to March

Foxlynch

Mr G H Edwins
Ogbourne St George, Marlborough
SN8 1TD
T: 01672 841307 **M:** 07855 909882
Bunkroom £20/person ⛹ 🔲 V ● ○
⚠ 🚲 👣
⛺ 20 £5/person 🚐 6 £5/person 🔲 🔥
🔥 ⓦ 🔲 🚲 **DRY** ◎
🕒 4 £12 🕓 4 £12
▌ Fee charged for transport to/from
Ridgeway. Horsebox parking available
for guests and day riders £5 per day

Grey Gables   *closed winter*   B&B

Ms Jeanette Therrien
Ogbourne St George,
Marlborough SN8 1SL
T: 01672 841464 **M:** 07977 053363
E: jet@jeanettetherrien.com
🛏 1 £60 (£45) ⛹(Min age 5) ♿ 🔲
V ● ○ 🚲 **DRY** Room en-suite

B&B | **Lavender House**

Mrs Jane Shave
High Street, Ogbourne St George,
Marlborough SN8 1SL
M: 07725 324869
E: lavenderhouse53@yahoo.com

🛏 1 £65 🛏 1 £40 ⚥ 📷 V ⚘ ● 🖉
🚲 **DRY** 🔘 👟 Some rooms en-suite

H | **Parklands Hotel**

Mark & Nicola Bentley
Ogbourne St George, Marlborough SN8
1SL
T: 01672 841555
E: mark@parklandshoteluk.co.uk
www.parklandshoteluk.co.uk

🛏/🛏 13 from £74 (£64) 🛏 1 £80
⚥ (min age 10) 🚻 V ● 🖉 🚫 🚲
DRY 🚗 👟 **VISA** Most major cards. All
rooms en-suite
🍴 Meals by advance booking

PARKLANDS HOTEL

Tel: 01672 841555
Email: mark@parklandshoteluk.co.uk
www.parklandshoteluk.co.uk

Mark & Nicola Bentley
welcome you to their hotel.
Comfortable accommodation,
cosy restaurant, bar and lounges,
to relax after your day's endurance.

New: two additional ground floor
bedrooms (adjoining) and
patio garden.

B&B | **Sanctuary**

Mrs Rebecca MacDonald
Ogbourne St George, Marlborough SN8
1SQ
T: 01672 841473
E: rebecca@the-sanctuary.biz
www.the-sanctuary.biz

🛏 1 £75 🛏 1 £75 (£58) 🛏 1 £110
⚥ 🚻 V ⚘ ○ 🖉 🚲 **DRY** 🔘 👟
Some rooms en-suite

Section 2

Ogbourne St George to Sparsholt Firs

Probably the most remote section of The Ridgeway, this 16 miles (25.6km) runs along the scarp face of the downs passing two Iron Age forts at Liddington and Uffington, the Stone Age long barrow of Wayland's Smithy and the wonderful figure of the Uffington White Horse. It also passes the only pub, at Fox Hill, directly on the western half of the Trail!

(Not to scale)

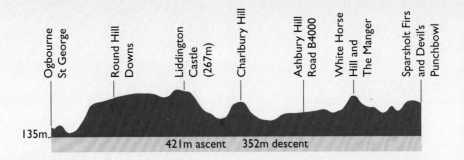

The elevation profile shows: Ogbourne St George, Round Hill Downs, Liddington Castle (267m), Charlbury Hill, Ashbury Hill Road B4000, White Horse Hill and The Manger, Sparsholt Firs and Devil's Punchbowl.

135m

421m ascent   352m descent

Maps

Landranger maps	174	Newbury and Wantage
Explorer maps	157	Marlborough and Savernake Forest
	170	Abingdon, Wantage and Vale of White Horse

Taxis

Place	Name	Telephone Number
Lambourn	Ray's	01488 71819
East Challow	Bonny's Taxis	07753 165890
Wantage	Cab Co	01235 772424
	Chapel Cars	07789 551931
	Evenlode Taxis	01235 762035
	Grove Cabs	01235 772200
	Keith's of Wantage	01235 763344
	Stuart's Taxis	01235 770608
	Webb's of Wantage	07881 647777

Car Parking

If you choose to park in villages close to The Ridgeway, please park considerately. Other places to park are listed below but you need to be aware that theft from cars parked in the countryside does occur. You are advised to leave any unnecessary items at home or, failing that, ensure that anything valuable is locked in the boot of your vehicle.

Place	Map Grid Reference
On Ridgeway at Fox Hill near Wanborough, 200m north-east of Shepherds Rest on road to Hinton Parva	SU 233814
On Ridgeway ½ mile (1km) south-east of Ashbury on B4000	SU 274844
National Trust car park for Uffington White Horse, south off B4507, ½ mile (700m) north of The Ridgeway	SU 293866
On Ridgeway at Sparsholt Firs on the south side of B4001, 2½ miles (4km) south of Childrey	SU 344851

Water Points

* with troughs for animals

Place	Map Grid Reference
Elm Tree Cottage, Southend (please ask before using)	SU 198734
Idstone Barn, Ashbury* (summer only - this supply comes from a private reservoir and can be intermittent. Fill bottle immediately as it may run dry after a few seconds)	SU 263835
Hill Barn, Sparsholt Firs* (April-Nov)	SU 338854

Vets

* large animal vets

Place	Name	Telephone Number
Swindon	Eastcott Veterinary Hospital	01793 528341
	The Drove Veterinary Hospital*	01793 522483
	Thameswood Veterinary Clinic	01793 511267
Lambourn	Valley Equine Hospital*	01488 71999
Faringdon	Danetree Veterinary Surgeons	01367 242777
	Elms Veterinary Surgery	01367 242416
Wantage	Abivale Veterinary Group	01235 770333
	Danetree Veterinary Surgeons	01235 770227

Farriers

Place	Name	Telephone Number
Uffington	Mervyn Richings	01367 820253
Lambourn	Alex Campbell	07702 126620
	AJ Charles	01488 71310
	Ben Joseph Elcock	07881 498703
	Thomas Garrett	07899 917300
	James A Stewart	01488 208243
	Benjamin Tillett	07832 267679
Ashbury	Terry Gill	07769 971333

Saddlers

Place	Name	Telephone Number
Lambourn	E J Wicks	01488 71766
Goosey	Asti Equestrian	01367 710288
Challow Station	Horse Shoe Saddlery	01367 710797
Childrey	White Horse Animal Feeds (no tack)	01235 751529

Riding Stables for Guided Rides

Place	Name	Telephone Number
Hinton Parva	Charlbury Farm Stables	01793 790065
Baulking	Baulking Grange	01367 718678

Horsebox Parking

The following places have sufficient space for you to park your horsebox. You **must** call in advance to arrange as space may be scarce. A fee may also be charged.

Place	Name	Telephone Number
Sparsholt Down	Down Barn Farm (Accommodation guests and day-riders)	01367 820272
Sparsholt Firs	Hill Barn (Accommodation guests and day-riders)	01235 751236

Bike Repairs

Place	Name	Telephone Number
Swindon	Mitchell Cycles	01793 523306
	Swindon Cycles Superstore	01793 700105
	Bike Doctor	01793 874873
	Total Bike	01793 644185
Wantage	Ridgeway Cycles	01235 764445
	GMC	01235 764204

Mountain Bike Hire

Place	Name	Telephone Number
Swindon	Swindon Cycles Superstore	01793 700105

Visitor Information Centres

These VICs are staffed but note that many libraries in the area also have leaflets about local attractions and events.

★ offers accommodation booking service

Place	Address/Opening Hours
★ Swindon	Central Library, Regents Circus, Swindon SN1 1QG **T**: 01793 466454 **E**: infocentre@swindon.gov.uk www.visitwiltshire.co.uk/swindon Opening hours: All year: Mon-Fri 09:30-17:00, Sat 09:30-16:00
★ Faringdon	The Corn Exchange, Corn Market, Faringdon SN7 7JA **T**: 01367 242191 **E**: tic@faringdontowncouncil.gov.uk www.faringdontowncouncil.gov.uk Opening hours: Mon-Fri 9:00-14:00, Sat 9:30-13:00
★ Wantage	Vale and Downland Museum & Visitor Centre 19 Church Street, Wantage OX12 8BL **T**: 01235 760176 **E**: tourism@wantage.com Opening hours: All year: Mon-Sat 10:00-16:00

Dragon Hill Towards White Horse Hill

41

ALDBOURNE

SU2675 ⌂ 3.3 miles (5.2km)
🚉 Swindon 10 miles (16km) 🚻
♿WC

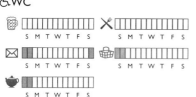

🅰 in Post Office and Co-op
Pub: Blue Boar 01672 540237 &
Crown 01672 540214

Crown at Aldbourne

Mr Alan Walters
2 The Square, Aldbourne, Marlborough
SN8 2DU
T: 01672 540214
E: bookings@thecrownaldbourne.co.uk
www.thecrownaldbourne.co.uk
🛏 3 £75 🛏 1 £60 🎎 ✉ V 🍎 O
🎨 🚗 🚲 💳 Most major cards.
★★★ All rooms en-suite

LIDDINGTON

SU2081 ⌂ 0.6 miles (1km)
🚉 Swindon 4 miles (7km)

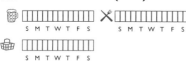

Pub: Village Inn 01793 790314

☆ Liddington Castle
www.themodernantiquarian.com

Meadowbank House   B&B

Mrs Jane Howes
Meadbourne Lane, Liddington, SN4 0EY
T: 01793 791401 **M:** 07951 563367
E: jhowes@meadowbankhouse.com
www.meadowbankhouse.com
🛏 3 £50 (£45) 🎎 🍎 O 🎨 🚲
DRY 🚗 🐕 💳 Most major cards.
Some rooms en-suite

Village Inn   INN

Mrs Donna Jones
Bell Lane, Liddington SN4 0HE
T: 01793 790314 **M:** 07877 691475
E: village28inn@btconnect.com
www.villageinn-liddington.co.uk
🛏 1 £60 (£50) 🛏 1 £60 (£50)
🛏 1 £80 🎎 (min age 8) V 🍎 O 🎨 🌙
🚲 **DRY** 🚗 🐕 💳 All major cards.
Some rooms en-suite

WANBOROUGH

SU2182 ⌂ 1.2 miles (2km)
🚉 Swindon 4 miles (7km)

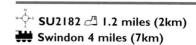
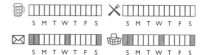

🅰 in Post Office

BISHOPSTONE

SU2483 👟 **0.6 miles (1km)**

🚂 **Swindon 7 miles (11km)**

🍺 ▯▯▯▯▯▯▯▯▯▯▯▯ ✗ ▮▯▯▯▯▯▯▯▯▯▯▯
S M T W T F S   S M T W T F S

Pub: Royal Oak 01793 790481

Cheney Thatch

Bishopstone, Swindon, Wiltshire
Tel 01793 790508

16th Century stone thatched cottage
in unique peaceful setting.
Trout stream through garden,
summer marquee. Heated outdoor
swimming pool. Footpath to
Ridgeway from garden gate.

Cheney Thatch	B&B

Mrs R Boot
Oxon Place, Bishopstone, Swindon
SN6 8PS
T: 01793 790508

🛏 2 £55 (£45) ⛄ (min age 8) 🐾 **V**
● O 🚲 🚲 **DRY** 🔟 🚗 ★★★ All
rooms have own bathroom

Royal Oak	

Mr Tim Finney
Cues Lane, Bishopstone, Swindon
SN6 8PP
T: 01793 790481
E: royaloak@helenbrowningorganics.
co.uk
www.helenbrowningorganics.co.uk

🛏 2 £75 (£45) 🛏 1 £110 ⛄ ♿
🐾 **V** ● ● 🚲 🚲 🚗 🚗 **VISA** Most
major cards. All rooms en-suite
🍴 Book evening meal in advance. Most
food provided is grown on our own
organic farm.

ASHBURY

 SU2685 🥾 **0.6 miles (1km)**

🚃 **Swindon 8 miles (13km)**

S M T W T F S   S M T W T F S

Pub: Rose & Crown Hotel 01793 710222

☆ Ashdown House
T: 01793 762209
www.nationaltrust.org.uk

Rose & Crown

Gavin Ingram
3 High Street, Ashbury, Swindon
SN6 8NA
T: 01793 710222
E: bookings@roseandcrowninn.co.uk
www.roseandcrowninn.co.uk

🛏 3 £70 🛏 2 £70 🛏 1 £130 🛏 2
£55 🎎 ♿ 📺 V ♥ ○ 🎨 🜂 ⬮ **DRY**
🚶 📶 💳 Most major cards. All rooms
en-suite

ROSE & CROWN INN

www.roseandcrowninn.co.uk
bookings@roseandcrowninn.co.uk

The Rose and Crown Inn is a 16th century coaching inn located in the heart of Ashbury village, Oxfordshire. Just ½ a mile from the Ridgeway National Trail.

A family friendly local, you can relax in the bar and dining areas with open fires or try the patio terrace and garden enjoying the scenic views. Enjoy our lunch and dinner menus prepared by Paul and his team from seasonal locally sourced ingredients.

Extensively refurbished in February 2013, the Rose & Crown Inn has eight en-suite bedrooms and a function / games room with pool table, computer games, TV and table tennis table.

Book online to access our best rates and promotional offers or contact us direct by telephone or email. So if you would like a little more than just a dining experience, come and enjoy a visit at The Rose & Crown. We look forward to welcoming you.

**3 HIGH STREET,
ASHBURY,
OXFORDSHIRE,
SN6 8NA.
T: 01793 710222**

WOOLSTONE

SU2987 👢 **1.2 miles (2km)**
🚂 **Swindon 11 miles (18km)**

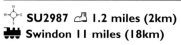

Pub: White Horse Inn 01367 820726

🛏 White Horse

Mr Keith Adams
Woolstone, Faringdon SN7 7QL
T: 01367 820726 **M:** 07818 257154
E: info@whitehorsewoolstone.co.uk
www.whitehorsewoolstone.co.uk
🛏 4 £85 🛏 2 £85 (£70) 🛏 1 £140
🛏 6 £70 ✝ 📷 V 🍎 O 🔥 🚫 🚲
DRY 🚗 📶 💳 Most major cards All rooms en-suite

UFFINGTON

SU3089 👢 **1.9 miles (3km)**
🚂 **Swindon 12 miles (19km) P F**

Open summer only

Pub: Fox & Hounds 01367 820680

☆ Tom Brown's School Museum
www.museum.uffington.net.

☆ Uffington White Horse and Castle
T: 01793 762209
www.nationaltrust.org.uk

Fox and Hounds 🛏

Mrs Janet Kirk
High Street, Uffington SN7 7RP
T: 01367 820680
E: enquiries@uffingtonpub.co.uk
www.uffingtonpub.co.uk
🛏 / 🛏 / 🛏 2 from £87 (£73) ✝
♿ 📷 V 🍎 🔥 🚫 🚲 DRY 📶 💳
Most major cards ★★★★ All rooms en-suite
🔔 No evening meals on Sunday but lift available to local pub

Norton House B&B

Mrs Fenella Oberman
Broad Street, Uffington, Faringdon SN7 7RA
T: 01367 820230
E: carloberman123@btinternet.com
www.smoothhound.co.uk/hotels/nortonfaringdon
🛏 1 £65 (£50) 🛏 / 🛏 1 £65 🛏 1 £40 ✝ 📷 V 🍷 O 🔥 🚲 DRY 🔘 📶
★★★★
🔔 VisitEngland Silver Award and Breakfast Award. Private bathrooms. Small donation for transport to/from Ridgeway or to pub for evening meal

▲ Britchcombe Countryside Holidays

⊹ SU307873 ½ mile from Ridgeway
Mrs Marcella Seymour
Britchcombe Farm, Uffington, Faringdon
SN7 7QJ
T: 01367 821022
E: campsite@britchcombefarm.co.uk
www.britchcombefarm.co.uk
🏕 30 £7/person 🚐 20 £7/person 🚻

🛏 Yurt and tipi available for hire.
Children 5-14 half price, under 5s free.
Tearoom summer weekends

KINGSTON LISLE

⊹ **SU3287** 👢 **1.2 miles (2km)**
🚆 **Swindon 14 miles (22km)**

🍺								✕							
S	M	T	W	T	F	S		S	M	T	W	T	F	S

Pub: Blowingstone Inn 01367 820288

SPARSHOLT

⊹ **SU3487** 👢 **1.9 miles (3km)**
🚆 **Didcot 12 miles (20km)**

🍺								✕							
S	M	T	W	T	F	S		S	M	T	W	T	F	S

Pub: Star Inn 01235 751873

Hill Barn Farmhouse — B&B

⊹ SU338852 100m S of Ridgeway
Mrs Joanna Whittington
Sparsholt Firs, Wantage OX12 9XB
T: 01235 751236 **M:** 07885 368918
E: jmw@hillbarn.plus.com
www.hillbarnbedandbreakfast.co.uk
🛏 1 £80 🛏 1 £80 (£45) 🚻 ▨ V
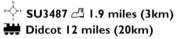 ★★★ All
rooms en-suite
🏕 5 £5/person ▨ 🚰 🚿 🚾 ♿ 🚲
DRY ▨
Ⓢ 5 £15 Ⓖ 5 £5
🛏 Free horsebox parking for guests and
day riders

Down Barn Farm — B&B

⊹ GR SU333851 900m S of Ridgeway ▲
Mrs P A Reid
Sparsholt Down, Wantage OX12 9XD
T: 01367 820272 **M:** 07799 833115
E: pendomeffect@aol.com
🛏 1 £80 🛏 2 £75 (£45) 🚻 ♿
 Some
rooms en-suite
🏕 4 £5/person ▨ 🚰 🚿 🚾 ▨ 🚲
DRY ▨
Ⓢ 2 £12 Ⓖ 4 £5
🛏 Evening meals not available every
Sunday. Call in advance to arrange
horsebox parking. Free horsebox
parking for day riders

Hill Barn B&B Farmhouse
Tel 01235 751236
E: jmw@hillbarn.plus.com

Uniquely situated just 100m from The Ridgeway at Sparsholt Firs.

In a secluded position but with panoramic views of both the Vale of White Horse and the Lambourn Downs, near the Uffington White Horse.

Walkers, riders and cyclists will enjoy a very friendly welcome with tea, an optional evening meal and packed lunch with home grown or local produce.

Free WiFi internet connection. Conservatory/TV lounge.

Star Inn — *closed 2 weeks mid Jan*

Dave Watts
Watery Lane, Sparsholt, Wantage OX12 9PL
T: 01235 751873
E: info@thestarsparsholt.co.uk
www.thestarsparsholt.co.uk

6 £95 (£75)   2 £95 (£75)
1 £75   Most major cards. All rooms en-suite
£10 charge for dogs. No evening meals Sunday and Monday

Crab apple

Linseed near Sparsholt Firs

Autumn ploughing

Section 3

Sparsholt Firs to Streatley

This 17.4 miles (27.9km) stretch keeps to the high scarp edge before losing height towards the end as it drops into the Thames Valley. It includes the widest parts of the Trail and some of the best conditions underfoot. This is racehorse country with gallops alongside the Trail in many places.

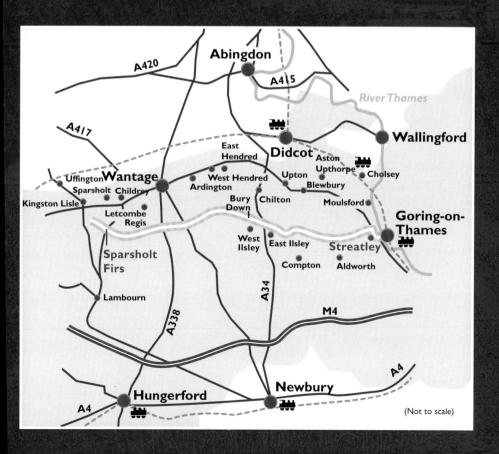

(Not to scale)

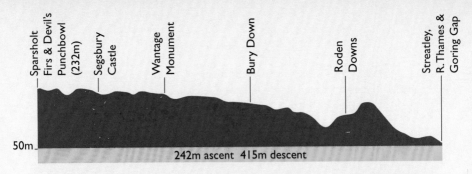

242m ascent 415m descent

Maps

Landranger maps	174	Newbury and Wantage
Explorer maps	170	Abingdon, Wantage and Vale of White Horse

Taxis

Place	Name	Telephone Number
East Challow	Grove Cabs	01235 772200
	Bonny's Taxis	07753 165890
Wantage	Cab Co	01235 772424
	Chapel Cars	07789 551931
	Evenlode Taxis	01235 762035
	Keith's of Wantage	01235 763344
	Stuart's Taxis	01235 770608
	Webb's of Wantage	07881 647777
Aston Upthorpe	Astons Airport Services	07837 343680

Car Parking

If you choose to park in villages close to The Ridgeway, please park considerately. Other places to park are listed below but you need to be aware that theft from cars parked in the countryside does occur. You are advised to leave any unnecessary items at home or, failing that, ensure that anything valuable is locked in the boot of your vehicle.

Place	Map Grid Reference
On Ridgeway at Sparsholt Firs on the south side of B4001, 2½ miles (4km) south of Childrey	SU 344851
On Ridgeway on the east side of B4494, 3 miles (5km) south of Wantage	SU 418841
On Ridgeway at Scutchamer's Knob, 2 miles (3km) south of East Hendred off the A417 east of Wantage	SU 458851
On Ridgeway at Bury Down on minor road from A34 to West Ilsley (signed Ridgeway from A34)	SU 479841
On Ridgeway at end of Rectory Road, Streatley, west off A417	SU 567813

Water Points

* with troughs for animals

Place	Map Grid Reference
Hill Barn, Sparsholt Firs*	SU 338854
The Court Hill Ridgeway Centre (YHA), Letcombe Regis*	SU 393849
Compton Downs*	SU 506828

Toilets

Place	Map Grid Reference
The Court Hill Ridgeway Centre (YHA), Letcombe Regis	SU 393849

Vets

* large animal vets

Place	Name	Telephone Number
Lambourn	Valley Equine Hospital*	01488 71999
Wantage	Abivale Veterinary Group	01235 770333
	Danetree Veterinary Surgeons	01235 770227
Cholsey	Larkmead Veterinary Group*	01491 651379
	- for equine	01491 651479
Goring-on-Thames	The Goring Veterinary Centre	01491 873638

Farriers

Place	Name	Telephone Number
Wantage	GP Feltham	07768 637068
	RGD Godfrey	07921 257012
	TD Godfrey	01235 868492
Blewbury	Ian Belcher	01235 850029

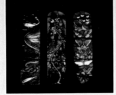

Saddlers

Place	Name	Telephone Number
Challow Station	Horse Shoe Saddlery	01367 710797
Childrey	White Horse Animal Feeds (no tack)	01235 751529
Denchworth	Denchworth Equestrian Supplies	01235 886175
Blewbury	Total Equestrian	01235 850188

Riding Stables for Guided Riding

Place	Name	Telephone Number
Blewbury	Blewbury Centre	01235 851016

Horsebox Parking

The following places have sufficient space for you to park your horsebox. You **must** call in advance to arrange as space may be scarce. A fee may also be charged.

Place	Name	Telephone Number
Blewbury	Blewbury Centre	01235 851016
Sparsholt Firs	Hill Barn (Accommodation guests and day-riders)	01235 751236
Upton	Prospect House (Accommodation guests and day-riders)	01235 850268

Bike Repairs

Place	Name	Telephone Number
Wantage	Ridgeway Cycles	01235 764445
	GMC	01235 764204
Abingdon	Behind Bars Cycle Shop	01235 533287
	Pedal Power Cycles	01235 525123
Didcot	Mountain Mania	01235 759366
Goring-on-Thames	Mountain Mania	01491 871721

Mountain Bike Hire

Place	Name	Telephone Number
Abingdon	Behind Bars	01235 533287
Goring-on-Thames	Mountain Mania	01491 871721

Tourist Information Centres

These TICs are staffed but note that many libraries in the area have leaflets about local attractions and events.

★ offers accommodation booking service

Place	Address/Opening Hours
★ Wantage	Vale and Downland Museum & Visitor Centre 19 Church Street, Wantage OX12 8BL **T**: 01235 760176 **E**: tourism@wantage.com Opening hours: All year: Mon-Sat 10:00-16:00
Abingdon-on-Thames	Visitor & Community Information Centre, The Guildhall, Abbey Close, Abingdon OX14 3JD **T**: 01235 522711 **E**: information@abingdon.gov.uk www.abingdon.gov.uk Opening hours: Mon-Fri 09:00-17:00 (closed Bank Holidays) Sat 10:00-15:00 (Oct-May) Sat 10:00-16:00 (June Sep)

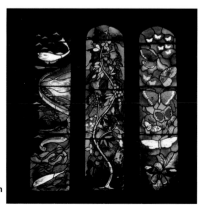

John Piper window in
Farnborough church

LETCOMBE REGIS

 **SU3886** 🐾 **1.2 miles (0.7km)**
🚉 **Didcot 10 miles (16km)**

🍺							✕						
S	M	T	W	T	F	S	S	M	T	W	T	F	S

Pub: Greyhound Inn 01235 764960

▲ 🏕 Court Hill Centre

The Manager
Court Hill, Letcombe Regis, Wantage
OX12 9NE
T: 01235 760253
E: info@courthill.org.uk
www.courthill.org.uk
🚻 ♿ V 🍴 🏞 🚫 🚲 **DRY** 🅿 **VISA** Most
major cards.
🏕 Several £8/person 🔌 🚿 🔥 ♿ 📋
🚲 **DRY** 🅿 **VISA** Most major cards
🛏 Dormitory and small family rooms
available from £18.50/person. Dogs on
leads at all times on campsite

B&B Quince Cottage

Mrs Louise Boden
Letcombe Regis, Wantage OX12 9JP
T: 01235 763652 **M:** 07853 906813
E: louise.boden@bodenfamily.info
www.bodenfamily.info
🛏 1 £75 🛏 1 £75 (£40) 🛏 1 £90
🛏 1 £40 🚻 🏠 V 🍴 ○ 🏞 🚲 **DRY** 🅿
🚗 🚶 Some rooms en-suite

WANTAGE

 **SU4088** 🐾 **2.5 miles (4km)**
🚉 **Didcot 8 miles (13km)** 🅸

Town with full range of services, visit
www.wantage.com for further details. It
has a wide range of accommodation -
details from Visitor Centre (see section
introduction). Farmers Market last
Saturday morning of each month.

☆ The Vale & Downland Museum
T: 01235 771447
www.wantage-museum.com.

ARDINGTON

 **SU4388** 🐾 **2.5 miles (4km)**
🚉 **Didcot 6 miles (10km)**

🍺							✕						
S	M	T	W	T	F	S	S	M	T	W	T	F	S

🧺							🫖						
S	M	T	W	T	F	S	S	M	T	W	T	F	S

🗞						
S	M	T	W	T	F	S

🅰 in shop
Pub: Boar's Head 01235 835466

☆ Ardington House (open summer
only) **T:** 01235 821566

WEST HENDRED

 **SU4488** 2.5 miles (4km)
Didcot 6 miles (9km)

S M T W T F S   S M T W T F S

Pub: Hare 01235 820383

EAST HENDRED

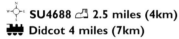 **SU4688** 2.5 miles (4km)
Didcot 4 miles (7km)

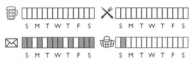
S M T W T F S   S M T W T F S

S M T W T F S   S M T W T F S

☆ Hendred Museum: April-Oct Sundays
14:30-16:30
T: 01235 833453
www.hendredmuseum.org.uk

☆ Hendred Vineyard
www.hendredvineyard.co.uk
01235 828430

B&B | Monk's Court

Mrs Susie Turnbull
Newbury Road, East Hendred, Wantage
OX12 8LG
T: 01235 833797 **M:** 07710 274653
E: susie@monkscourt.co.uk
www.monkscourt.co.uk

2 £74   1 £74 (£40) ★★★
Some rooms en-suite

Greensands Guest House | B&B

Ms Debbie Cox
Reading Road, East Hendred, Wantage
OX12 8JE
T: 01235 833338
E: debbie_740@hotmail.com
www.bed-and-breakfast-oxfordshire.co.uk

13 £80   1 £80   3 £90 (£60)
5 £60 ★★★   Most major cards.
Some rooms en-suite.
House ★★★ annexe ★★★★

WEST ILSLEY

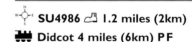 **SU4782** 1.2 miles (2km)
Didcot 7 miles (11km)

S M T W T F S   S M T W T F S

Pub: Harrow Inn 01635 281260

CHILTON

 **SU4986** 1.2 miles (2km)
Didcot 4 miles (6km) P F

S M T W T F S   S M T W T F S

S M T W T F S

Pub: Rose & Crown 01235 862992

EAST ILSLEY

SU4981  1.2 miles (2km)
Didcot 7 miles (11km)

Pubs: Crown and Horns 01635 281545
Swan Hotel 01635 281238

■ Crown & Horns Inn

Kim O'Brien
Compton Road, East Ilsley RG20 7LH
T: 01635 281545
E: info@crownandhorns.com
www.crownandhorns.com

8 £59 1 £65 **ii** & V ● O
● ● *VISA* Most major cards. All rooms
en-suite

■ Swan Hotel   *closed 24-2 Jan*

Mr Richard Vellender
High St, East Ilsley RG20 7LF
T: 01635 281238
E: kimrichstar@aol.com
www.theswaneastilsley.co.uk

2 £75 3 £69 (£69) **ii**(min
age 12) V ● ● ● ● **DRY** ● ●
VISA Most major cards. All rooms en-
suite
● Evening meals not available Sundays.
Multiple night breaks available, see
advert opposite

UPTON

SU5186  2.5 miles (4km)
Didcot 3 miles (5km)

Pub: George & Dragon 01235 850723
Food served only to 7pm Sunday

Prospect House   *closed Xmas* B&B

Mrs Hilary Powell
Upton, Didcot OX11 9HU
T: 01235 850268 **M:** 07966 205688
E: hilary_powell@btinternet.com
www.prospect-house.info

1 £75 1 £70 (£50) 1 £80
ii V ● O ● **DRY** ● ●
● 2 £15 ● 4 £5
● Free parking for guests' horseboxes
up to 7.5 tons

Clematis

Swan Hotel

East Ilsley
Tel 01635 281238
www.theswaneastilsley.co.uk

Traditional 17th century inn with with 5 en-suite bedrooms including a
four-poster suite. Richard and Kim have been welcoming users of
The Ridgeway to East Ilsley for over 10 years and have detailed
knowledge of the Trail from Overton Hill to Nuffield.
Read about us on Trip Advisor, Late Rooms.com and Booking.com.

Multiple night breaks from £50/night B&B. Phone for best price

COMPTON

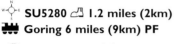

SU5280 1.2 miles (2km)
Goring 6 miles (9km) PF

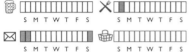

Pub: Compton Swan 01635 579400

| INN | **Compton Swan** | *closed 1 Jan* |

Greene King
High Street, Compton, Newbury
RG20 6NJ
T: 01635 579400
E: info@thecomptonswan.com
www.thecomptonswan.com
/ 6 £90 (£80) ♀♂ V ● ⅍
Some major cards.
★★★★ All rooms en-suite
Children under 5 free. Lift by arrangement

BLEWBURY

SU5385 2.5 miles (4km)
Didcot 4 miles (6km) PF

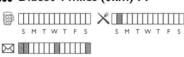

Pub: Red Lion 01235 850403

Blewbury Centre

Miss Jane Dexter
Besselsway, Blewbury OX11 9NH
T: 01235 851016
M: 07809 040914 (text only)
E: info@blewburycentre.co.uk
www.blewburycentre.co.uk
5 £10 5 £10 ♀♂
(S) £15 (G) £10
Café open Saturdays and competition days 10am-4pm. Horsebox parking free for dayriders

Red Lion INN

Bob and Sandra Hurst
Chapel Lane, Blewbury OX11 9PQ
T: 01235 850403
E: redlionblewbury@yahoo.co.uk
www.redlionblewbury.vpweb.co.uk
/ 1 £75 (£65) ♀♂ V ● ⅍
DRY Most major cards.
Room is en-suite
No evening meal Sundays.

Yew Tree B&B

Mrs Liz Thacker
London Road, Blewbury OX11 9PF
T: 01235 850678
E: lizthackeryewtree@hotmail.com
1 £50 1 £45 V ● ⅍ DRY
One room en-suite

ASTON UPTHORPE

 SU5986 **3.3 miles (5.3km)**
🚃 **Didcot 3.7 miles (5.9km)**

S M T W T F S   S M T W T F S

Pub/restaurant: Sweet Olive 01235 851272
(closed 3 weeks Feb and 2 weeks in July)

B&B | Middle Fell

Mrs Christine Millin
Moreton Road, Aston Upthorpe,
Didcot OX11 9ER
T: 01235 850207 **M:** 07833 920678
E: middlefell@ic24.net
www.middlefell.co.uk
🛏 1 £65 🛏 2 £65 (£45) 🛏 1 £130
👪 V 🟡 🚲 ★★★★ All rooms
en-suite

ALDWORTH

 SU5579 🥾 **1.2 miles (2km)**
🚃 **Goring 3 miles (5km)**

S M T W T F S   S M T W T F S

S M T W T F S   S M T W T F S

Pubs: Bell 01635 578272 & Four Points
01635 578367
www.aldworth.info
Saturday morning weekly market

MOULSFORD

 SU5983 🥾 **1.2 miles (2km)**
🚃 **Cholsey 2 miles (3km)**

S M T W T F S   S M T W T F S

Pub: Beetle & Wedge 01491 651381

Beetle & Wedge Boathouse B&B

Mrs Stephanie Musk
Ferry Lane, Moulsford OX10 9JF
T: 01491 651381
E: boathouse@beetleandwedge.co.uk
www.beetleandwedge.co.uk
🛏 3 £90 🛏 2 £90 (£75) 👪 V 🟡
🟡 🔥 🟦 **DRY** 🔘 🚶 **VISA** All major cards.
★★★★ All rooms en-suite

Blackthorn

Streatley-on-Thames

 SU5980 on path

Goring & Streatley 0.5 miles (1km)

S M T W T F S   S M T W T F S

Pubs: Swan at Streatley 01491 878800 & Bull at Streatley 01491 872392

☆ The Holies Nature Reserve
T: 0118 984 3040

☆ Basildon Park
T: 0118 984 3040
www.nationaltrust.org.uk

☆ Beale Wildlife Park
T: 0844 826 1761 www.bealepark.co.uk

Hogweed

Swan at Streatley

The Manager
High Street, Streatley RG8 9HR
T: 01491 878800
E: reservations@theswanatstreatley.com
www.theswanatstreatley.com

27 £125 7 £125 (£115) 5 £99 All major cards. All rooms en-suite
Any cot or extra bed £20/night. Dogs £10/night

Bull at Streatley

Miss Emma Brooks
Reading Road, Streatley RG8 9JJ
T: 01491 872392
E: thebullatstreatley@hotmail.co.uk
www.bullstreatley.com

3 2 £70 (£60) Most major cards. All rooms en-suite
No meals after 6pm on Sundays

YHA Streatley

Mr Nick Crivich
Hill House, Reading Road, Streatley RG8 9JJ
T: 01491 872278
E: streatley@yha.org.uk
www.yha.org.uk

2 £25 8 £40 Most major cards ★★★
WiFi available

B&B **3 Icknield Cottages**

Mrs Susan Brodie
High Street, Streatley RG8 9JA
T: 01491 875152 **M:** 07989 152295
🛏 1 £30 V 🍎 ● ⬥ 🚲 **DRY** 🔲

SC **Linden Cottage - Old Stables and the Annexe**

Mrs Sue Jubb
Streatley RG8 9NB
T: 01491 871120 **M:** 07747 388957
E: sue_jubb@hotmail.com
www.lindencottages.co.uk
👪 ♿ 🚲 **DRY** 🔲
🅷 Self-catering £45/night, £295/week

Linksdown Studio **B&B SC** ♘

Mrs Gaye Walsh
Rectory Road, Streatley RG8 9QA
T: 01491 873139
E: gayewalsh@gmail.com
www.linksdownbedandbreakfast.com
🛏 1 £75 V 🍎 ● 🚲 🚗 🧍
Room is en-suite
🅖 2 £10
🅷 Self-catering £65/night, min 2 nights.
Pick up from station by arrangement

Stable Cottages **B&B** ♘

Mrs Diana Fenton
Wallingford Road, Streatley RG8 9JX
T: 01491 874408
🛏 1 £60 (£30) 🛏 1 £30 👪 (min age
10) V 🍎 O ⬥ 🚲 **DRY** 🔲 🧍
🅢 2 £15

After harvest near Streatley

Brunel's Bridge, north of South Stoke

Grim's Ditch east of Wallingford during Spring

Section 4

Streatley to Watlington

At the start of this 15.3 miles (24.6km) section The Ridgeway crosses another National Trail, the Thames Path, before following the bank of the River Thames for a few picturesque miles. The Trail then heads east into the more wooded Chilterns via an ancient Grim's Ditch and finishes on the wide track of the old Icknield Way.

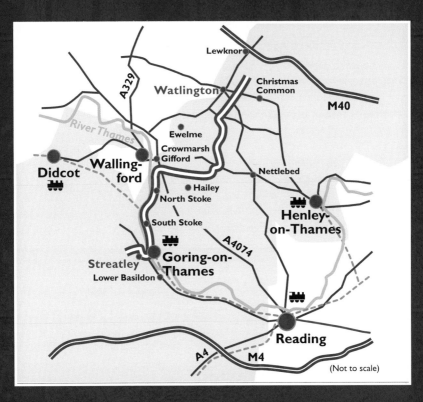

(Not to scale)

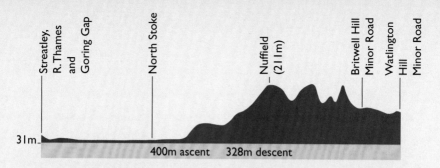

Maps

Landranger maps	174	Newbury and Wantage
	175	Reading and Windsor
Explorer maps	171	Chiltern Hills West

Taxis

Place	Name	Telephone Number
Goring-on-Thames	Airpal Taxis	07862 721698
Wallingford	Hills Taxis	01491 837022
Nettlebed	Andy Hearn Private Hire	01491 641159

Car Parking

If you choose to park in villages close to The Ridgeway, please park considerately. Other places to park are listed below but you need to be aware that theft from cars parked in the countryside does occur. You are advised to leave any unnecessary items at home or, failing that, ensure that anything valuable is locked in the boot of your vehicle.

Place	Map Grid Reference
Goring-on-Thames public car park	SU 599807
On Ridgeway on west side of minor road, 1 mile (1½km) from Britwell Salome heading southeast	SU 681922
On Ridgeway on east side of Hill Road, minor road to Christmas Common ½ mile (1km) southeast of Watlington	SU 698940

Water Points

Place	Map Grid Reference
Grimsdyke Cottage, Grim's Ditch	SU 660872
Church, Nuffield (on the wall)	SU 667874
White Mark Farm Camp Site, Watlington (March - Nov)	SU 697939

Toilets

Place	Map Grid Reference
Goring-on-Thames (Car Park off Station Road)	SU 602807
White Mark Farm Camp Site, Watlington (March - October)	SU 697939
Watlington (High Street) ♿	SU 689945

Vets

* large animal vets

Place	Name	Telephone Number
Goring-on-Thames	The Goring Veterinary Centre	01491 873638
Cholsey	Larkmead Veterinary Group* - for equine	01491 651379 01491 651479
Wallingford	Abivale Veterinary Group	01491 839043
Watlington	Crossroads Veterinary Centre	01491 612799

Farriers

Place	Name	Telephone Number
Watlington	William Smith	01491 612872
	Adrian Spilsbury	07968 065991
Nettlebed	Andrew Speller	079589 93557

Saddlers

Place	Name	Telephone Number
Blewbury	Total Equestrian	01189 714554

Horsebox Parking

The following places have sufficient space for you to park your horsebox. You **must** call in advance to arrange as space may be scarce. A fee may also be charged.

Place	Name	Telephone Number
Ewelme	Mays Farms (Accommodation guests and day-riders)	01491 642056

Bike Repairs

Place	Name	Telephone Number
Goring-on-Thames	Mountain Mania	01491 871721
Wallingford	Rides on Air	01491 836289
Thame	2 Wheels	01844 212455
	Thame Cycles	01844 261520

Mountain Bike Hire

Place	Name	Telephone Number
Goring-on-Thames	Mountain Mania	01491 871721

Visitor Information Centres

This VIC is staffed but note that many libraries in the area also have leaflets about local attractions and events.

Place	Address/Opening Hours
Wallingford	Wallingford Town Information Centre, Town Hall, Market Place, Wallingford OX10 0EG

T: 01491 826972 **E:** tic@wallingfordtc.co.uk
www.wallingford.co.uk
Opening hours:
Mar to mid Dec: Mon to Fri 10:00-16:00 (closed 12:30-13:00)
Sat 10:00-14:00
Mid-Dec to Feb: Mon to Sat 10:00-14:00 (closed Bank Hols)

View over Goring-on-Thames

LOWER BASILDON

 **SU6078** **1.6 miles (2.7km)**
🚆 **Goring & Streatley 1.2 miles (2km)**

✉ 🔲🔲🔲🔲🔲🔲🔲🔲🔲🔲🔲
S M T W T F S

T: 01491 671555

☆ Basildon Park
T: 0118 984 3040
www.nationaltrust.org.uk

B&B ▌Grove House

Sue Trevor Wilson
Reading Road, Lower Basildon RG8 9ND
T: 01491 875939 **M:** 07833 920678
E: suetrevorwilson@sky.com
🛏 2 £70 (£60) 👫 (5 years min)
🍷🄾 🚗 📶
▌ Payment by Paypal

GORING-ON-THAMES

 **SU6080** **on path**
🚆 **Goring & Streatley P£** Ⓜ
♿WC

🍺 🔲🔲🔲🔲🔲🔲🔲🔲🔲🔲🔲   ✕ 🔲🔲🔲🔲🔲🔲🔲🔲🔲🔲🔲
S M T W T F S   S M T W T F S

✉ ▌🔲🔲🔲🔲🔲🔲🔲🔲🔲🔲   🧺🔲🔲🔲🔲🔲🔲🔲🔲🔲🔲🔲
S M T W T F S   S M T W T F S

🫖 ▌🔲🔲🔲🔲🔲🔲🔲🔲🔲🔲   ✉ ▌🔲🔲🔲🔲🔲🔲🔲🔲🔲🔲
S M T W T F S   S M T W T F S

🎁 🔲🔲🔲🔲🔲🔲🔲🔲🔲🔲🔲
S M T W T F S

£ HSBC 🏧, Lloyds TSB
www.goring-on-thames.co.uk

▌John Barleycorn

Stephen Clay and Monika Arbaniak
Manor Road, Goring-on-Thames
RG8 9DP
T: 01491 872509 **E:** johnbarleycorn-goring@btconnect.com
www.thejohnbarleycornpub.com
🛏 3 £75 👫 (min age 12) 🄾 V 🍎 🌾
🄾 🚲 📶 💳 Most major cards. All rooms en-suite
▌ No evening meals on Sundays

▌Melrose Cottage   **B&B**

Mrs Rosemary Howarth
36 Milldown Road, Goring-on-Thames
RG8 0BD
T: 01491 873040 **M:** 07798 663897
E: melrose-cottage@goring-on-thames.co.uk
🛏 2 £60 🛏 1 £35 👫 (min age 5) V
🌾 🚲 **DRY** 🄾 🚗 📶

▌Miller of Mansfield

Manager: Arron Christopher
High Street, Goring-on-Thames RG8 9AW
T: 01491 872829
E: reservations@millerofmansfield.com
www.millerofmansfield.com
🛏 12 £85 🛏 1 £110 (£70) 🛏 2 £180 👫 🄾 V 🍎 🄾 🌾 🄾 🚲 📶
💳 All major cards. All rooms en-suite

B&B | Southview House

Dawn and Richard Roberts
Farm Road, Goring-on-Thames RG8 0AA
T: 01491 872184 **M:** 07957 571620
E: goringbnb@rglroberts.com
🛏/🛌 3 £70 (£65) ⚤ 🖼 V ● O
🚲 DRY 🗇 🛜 2 private bathrooms
✦ Min stay 2 nights/1 room or 1 night/2 rooms only

SOUTH STOKE

⊕ **SU5983** 👢 on path
🚂 **Goring & Streatley 2 miles (3km)**

Pub: Perch & Pike 01491 872415

INN | Perch & Pike

Kim Koniotes
The Street, South Stoke, Reading RG8 0JS
T: 01491 872415
E: hello@perchandpike.co.uk
www.perchandpike.co.uk
🛏 3 £95 🛌 1 £95 ⚤ 🖼 V ♦ 🍎 🍷
DRY 💳 Some major cards. ★★★ All rooms en-suite.
✦ No evening meals on Sundays.

Oak Barn | B&B

Mrs Vanessa Guiver
The Old Post Office, The Street, South Stoke, Reading RG8 0JS
T: 01491 871872 **M:** 07889 757767
E: info@oakbarn.org.uk
www.oakbarn.org.uk
🛏 1 £80 (£50) ⚤ (Min age 4) V ●
● 🍎 🚲 DRY 🗇 🚗 ♿ 🛜 Room is en-suite
✦ Extra charge for more than 2 people in room

NORTH STOKE

⊕ **SU6086** 👢 on path
🚂 **Goring & Streatley 4 miles (6km)**

Pub: Springs Hotel 01491 836687

Briar Cottage | B&B

Mrs Zazie Carruthers
1 The Street, North Stoke, Wallingford OX10 6BL
T: 01491 835833 **M:** 07969 462844
E: richardzazie@btinternet.com
🛏 1 £65 (£50) 🖼 V ♦ 🍎 🍷 🚲
DRY 🗇 Room is en-suite
✦ Evening meal by arrangement

Springs Hotel

Karolina Michalak
1 Wallingford Road, North Stoke,
Wallingford OX10 6BE
T: 01491 836687
E: reception@thespringshotel.com
www.thespringshotel.com

29 £110 3 £110 (£95)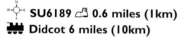
All major cards. All rooms en-suite

£15 supplement for children over 5 years

CROWMARSH GIFFORD

SU6189 0.6 miles (1km)
Didcot 6 miles (10km)

	S M T W T F S		S M T W T F S

Pubs: Queen's Head 01491 839857 &
Bell Pub (Hungry Horse) 01491 835324

☆ Riverside Park & Swimming Pool
T: 01491 835232

Wild Rose

Little Gables
B&B

Mrs Carole Baker
166 Crowmarsh Hill, Wallingford
OX10 8BG
T: 01491 837834
E: mail@littlegables.co.uk
www.littlegables.co.uk

3 £85 (£70) 3 £85 (£70)
1 £110 4 £70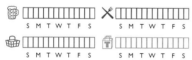
All major cards ★★★★ Some rooms en-suite

Lift available to local pub for evening meals

Bridge Villa Camping & Caravan Park
Campsite closed Jan
B&B

Mr Andrew Townsend
The Street, Crowmarsh Gifford,
Wallingford OX10 8HB
T: 01491 836860
E: bridge.villa@btconnect.com
www.bridgevilla.co.uk

1 £50 Most major cards. Room en-suite

Room only, no breakfast included

£16 £16 WC
 CG Most major cards

100 pitches in total

B&B Maran Cottage — closed Xmas

Mrs Christine Buckland-Jones
Old Reading Road, Crowmarsh Gifford,
Wallingford OX10 8EN
T: 01491 839122 **M:** 07952 865396
🛏 1 £60 (£50) V ● O ♿ 🚲 DRY
🚗 🚶 Room en-suite

🏕 Riverside Park — closed Oct - April

Josh Roper
The Street, Wallingford Bridge,
Crowmarsh Gifford, Wallingford
OX10 8EB
T: 01491 835232 (out of season 01865
341035)
E: riverside@gll.org
🏕 or 🚐 18 £15 🚿 ♨ ⏻ ♿ WC ▣
🚲

WALLINGFORD

⊕ **SU6089** 🥾 1.2 miles (2km)
🚂 **Cholsey 6 miles (9km)** 🚻

Town with full range of services, visit
www.wallingford.co.uk for further
details. Farmers Market 3rd Tues and
5th Sat morning of the month. Country
Market Friday mornings

☆ Wallingford Museum
T: 01491 835065
www.wallingfordmuseum.org.uk

☆ Wallingford Castle
www.berkshirehistory.com/castles/
wallingford_cast.html

George Hotel 🏠

Sarah Snell
High Street, Wallingford OX10 0BS
T: 01491 836665
E: rooms@george-hotel-wallingford.com
www.peelhotel.com
🛏 24 £115 🛏 4 £115 🛏 2 £140
(£110) 🛏 9 £98 ⚥ ♿ V ● ♿ ◐ 🚲
▣ 🛜 VISA Most major cards ★★★ All
rooms en-suite

11 St Leonards Lane — B&B

Carol Ferguson
11 St Leonards Lane, Wallingford OX10
0HA
T: 01491 833309 **M:** 07592 005113
E: carolferg@live.co.uk
🛏 1 £70 (£50) ⚥ V ● O 🛜 Private
bathroom

52 Blackstone Road — B&B

Mrs Enid Barnard
Wallingford OX10 8JL
T: 01491 839339
E: enid.barnard@googlemail.com
🛏 1 £50 (£35) 📷 V ● O 🚲 DRY
🚶

Old School House — closed Xmas week — B&B

Mrs Carolyn Bristow
23 Castle Street Wallingford OX10
8DW
T: 01491 839571 **M:** 07900 225167
E: bristow.carolyn@gmail.com
www.23oldschoolhouse.com
🛏 2 £85 🛏 1 £125 ⚥ V ● ● 🚲
DRY 🛜 Some rooms en-suite
🚻 Family price for 3 people

HAILEY

 **SU6485** 🥾 1.4 miles (2.3km)
🚂 Cholsey 5.3 miles (8.5km)

S M T W F S   S M T W F S

Pub: King William IV (Ipsden) 01491 681845

NETTLEBED

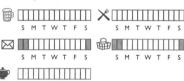 **SU70787** 🥾 2.9 miles (4.6km)
🚂 Henley-on-Thames 5.2 miles (8.4km) **P F**

🍺 | | | | | | | | | | | 🍴 | | | | | | | | | | |
S M T W F S   S M T W F S

✉ | | | | | | | | | | | 🧺 | | | | | | | | | | |
S M T W F S   S M T W F S

🫖 | | | | | | | | | | |
S M T W F S

Pub: White Hart Hotel 01491 641245

Ⓗ White Hart

The Manager
28 High Street, Nettlebed RG9 5DD
T: 01491 641245
E: whitehart@tmdining.co.uk
www.tmdining.co.uk

🛏 18 £80 🛏 1 £80 👫 👴 V 🍎 ♿
🅽 💳 All major cards ★★★★ All rooms en-suite
📶 🛜 in bar only

Wood Edge   B&B

Mr and Mrs Penny and David Waldie
44 Catslip, Nettlebed, Henley-on-Thames RG9 5BN
T: 01491 641354 **M:** 07780 703709
E: waldiepd@googlemail.com
www.bedandbreakfasthenley.co.uk

🛏 1 £70 🛏 1 £70 👫 (min age 2)
🔌 V 🍎 O ♿ 🚲 DRY 🔟 🚗 🚶
★★★★ All rooms en-suite

Somerset   B&B

Mrs Nan McDonnell
9 High Street, Nettlebed, Henley-on-Thames RG9 5DA
T: 01491 641710 **M:** 07854 531499
E: jandnmcd@greenbee.net
🛏 2 £70 (£35) V 🍴 🚲 DRY 🔟 🚗

EWELME

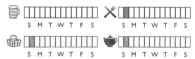 **SU6491** 🥾 1.3 miles (2.1km)
🚂 Henley-on-Thames 10.6 miles (17km) **P F**

🍺 | | | | | | | | | | | 🍴 | | | | | | | | | | |
S M T W F S   S M T W F S

🧺 | | | | | | | | | | | 🫖 | | | | | | | | | | |
S M T W F S   S M T W F S

Pub: Shepherd's Hut 01491 835636

☆ Ewelme Watercress Beds. Open first Sunday of month. T: 01494 835173
www.ewelmewatercressbeds.org

B&B SC | Fords Farm

Miss Marlene Edwards
Ewelme, Wallingford OX10 6HU
T: 01491 839272
E: fordsfarm@callnetuk.com
www.fordsfarm.co.uk

🛏 1 £80 🛏 2 £80 (£60) 👫 (min age 10) V 🍎 🦽 🚲 **DRY** 🚗 **VISA**
Mastercard, Visa. Some rooms en-suite
♺ VisitEngland Silver Award ★★★★
Self-catering unit: VisitEngland Gold Award ★★★★★ £165/night or £725/week

B&B | Mays Farm House

⌖ SU654885 1.3 miles (2.1km) from Ridgeway
Mrs Sue Veitch
Ewelme, Wallingford OX10 6QF
T: 01491 642056 **M:** 07791 121405
E: sue@maysfarmewelme.co.uk
www. maysfarmewelme.co.uk

🛏 1 £55 🛏 1 £35 👫 🖼 V 🍎 O 🦽
🚲 **DRY** 🚗 🧍
🍵 3 £10
♺ Lift to pubs/Ridgeway £3 each way. Free horsebox parking for guests and day-riders

Bluebells

WATLINGTON

✤ **SU6894** 🏳 **0.6 miles (1km)**
🚂 **Henley-on-Thames 10 miles (16km)** P F 👫 🦽WC
Small town with a range of services

☆ Watlington Hill and White Mark
www.nationaltrust.org.uk

Fat Fox Inn 🏛

Mr John Riddell
13 Shirburn Street, Watlington OX49 5BU
T: 01491 613040 **M:** 07788 920108
E: info@thefatfoxinn.co.uk
www.thefatfoxinn.co.uk

🛏 5 £89 🛏 4 £89 (£79) 👫 🖼
🦽 V 🍎 ● 🦽 🌐 📶 **VISA** Most major cards. All rooms en-suite

Woodgate Orchard Cottage | B&B

Ms Ronnie Roper
Howe Road, Watlington OX49 5EL
T: 01491 612675
E: ronnie.m.roper@gmail.com
🛏 3 £80 🛏 1 £80 (£50) 👫 🖼 V 🍎
O 🦽 🚲 **DRY** 🗑 🚗 🧍
♺ Charge for lift to/from Ridgeway

White Mark Farm   *closed 1 Dec-end Feb* ⛺

Mrs Debbie Bacon
82 Hill Road, Watlington OX49 5AF
T: 01491 612295
E: debbie.whitemarkfarm@yahoo.co.uk
www.whitemark.co.uk

⛺ 40 £6/person 🚐 5 £6/person 🖼 🚿
🚰 👫 🚽 🚲 **DRY**

Section 5

Watlington to Wendover

This 17 miles (27.2km) stretch is probably the most strenuous part of The Ridgeway. It starts out gently enough following the wide track of the Icknield Way but once it departs from this it climbs in and out of several Chilterns valleys. Passing through some lovely nature reserves the Trail reaches a high point with fantastic views at Coombe Hill before descending to Wendover. If you haven't already seen a red kite, you're guaranteed to see one on this stretch!

(Not to scale)

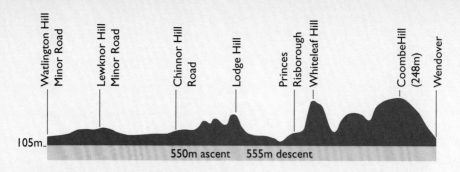

Watlington Hill / Minor Road · Lewknor Hill / Minor Road · Chinnor Hill / Road · Lodge Hill · Princes Risborough · Whiteleaf Hill · CoombeHill (248m) · Wendover

105m

550m ascent   555m descent

Maps

Landranger maps	175	Reading and Windsor
	165	Aylesbury and Leighton Buzzard
Explorer maps	171	Chiltern Hills West
	181	Chiltern Hills North

Taxis

Place	Name	Telephone Number
Chinnor	Thame & Chinnor Taxis	01844 353637
Loosley Row	Springline Cars	01844 274474
Princes Risborough	Risborough Cars	01844 274111
	Village Cars	01844 342551
	B&V Taxis	01844 342079
	Red Line Cars	01844 343736
Wendover	Alexander's	01296 620888

Car Parking

If you choose to park in villages close to The Ridgeway, please park considerately. Other places to park are listed below but you need to be aware that theft from cars parked in the countryside does occur. You are advised to leave any unnecessary items at home or, failing that, ensure that anything valuable is locked in the boot of your vehicle.

Place	Map Grid Reference
On Ridgeway on east side of Hill Road, minor road to Christmas Common ½ mile (1km) southeast of Watlington	SU 698940
On Ridgeway on east side of minor road to Bledlow Ridge ½ mile (1km) south of Chinnor	SP 761003
Princes Risborough public car park	SP 810034
Whiteleaf car park, ½ mile (1km) east of Princes Risborough. Turn right off A4010 at Monks Risborough and car park is on left at top of escarpment	SP 824036
National Trust car park for Coombe Hill, 1 mile (2km) southwest of Wendover. From Wendover travel west on minor road to Princes Risborough. Take first left, then first left again. At top of hill car park is on left	SP 852062
Wendover public car park	SP 868077

74

Water Points

Place	Map Grid Reference
White Mark Farm Camp Site, Watlington (March - October)	SU 697939
Aston Rowant National Nature Reserve (close to A40 Ridgeway crossing)	SU 727976

Toilets

Place	Map Grid Reference
Watlington (High Street)	SU 689945
White Mark Farm Camp Site, Watlington (March-November)	SU 697939
Chinnor Village Centre (High Street)	SP 757012
Princes Risborough (Horn Mill Car Park)	SP 809033
Wendover (Library Car Park)	SP 868078

Vets

Place	Name	Telephone Number
Watlington	Crossroads Veterinary Centre	01491 612799
Chinnor	Sprinz & Nash	01844 212000
Stokenchurch	Hall Place Veterinary Centre	01494 485855
Princes Risborough	Sprinz & Nash	01844 345655
Halton	Wendover Heights Veterinary Centre	01296 623439
Aylesbury	Hampden Veterinary Hospital*	01296 423666
	For equine	01296 745374

*Covers Watlington, Whiteleaf & Princes Risborough

Farriers

Place	Name	Telephone Number
Watlington	Adrian Spilsbury	07968 065991
Chinnor	DM Goth	07734 113045
	N Kilner	07867 521476
Stokenchurch	David Jennings	07877 324597
	John Jennings	07836 562784

Saddler

Place	Name	Telephone Number
Lacey Green	Widmer Feeds (no tack)	01844 344765
Speen, P Risborough	Beryl P Forrest	01494 488130

Bike Repairs

Place	Name	Telephone Number
Wallingford	Rides on Air	01491 836289
Thame	2 Wheels	01844 212455
	Thame Cycles	01844 261520
Great Missenden	Bicycle Mobile Workshop	01494 867358
		& 07973 530914

Mountain Bike Hire

Place	Name	Telephone Number
Princes Risborough	Risborough Cycles	01844 345949
Tring	Mountain Mania	01442 822458

Visitor Information Centres

★ offers accommodation booking service (until 15:30)

Place
Wallingford

Address/Opening Hours
Town Hall, Market Place, Wallingford OX10 0EG
T: 01491 826972 **E:** tic@wallingfordtc.co.uk
www.wallingford.co.uk
Opening hours:
Mar to mid Dec: Mon to Fri 10:00-16:00 (closed 12:30-13:00)
Sat 10:00-14:00
Mid-Dec to Feb: Mon to Sat 10:00-14:00 (closed Bank Hols)

Princes Risborough
Tower Court, Horns Lane, Princes Risborough HP27 0AJ
T: 01844 274795 www.visitbuckinghamshire.org.uk
E: risborough_office@wycombe.gov.uk
Opening hours: All year: Mon-Wed, Fri 09:00-17:00;
Thurs 10:00-17:00; Sat 09:00-13:00

★ Wendover
The Clock Tower, High Street, Wendover HP22 6DU
T: 01296 696759 **E:** tourism@wendover-pc.gov.uk
www.wendover-pc.gov.uk
Opening hours: All year: Mon, Thur, Fri, Sat 10:00-16:00

CHRISTMAS COMMON

 **SU7193** 🥾 **1.3 miles (2.1km)**
🚆 **Henley-on-Thames 9.6 miles (15.4km)**

S M T W T F S   S M T W T F S

Pub: Fox & Hounds 01491 612599

LEWKNOR

 **SU7197** 🥾 **0.6 miles (1km)**
🚆 **Princes Risborough 7 miles (12km)**

S M T W T F S   S M T W T F S

Pub: Leathern Bottle 01844 351482

B&B | **Moorcourt Cottage** | *Closed mid Dec to mid Mar*

Mrs Eppy Hodgson
Weston Road, Lewknor OX49 5RU
T: 01844 351419
E: moorcourt2002@yahoo.co.uk
🛏 1 £72 🛏 1 £72 (£47) ⚥ V ♿
○ 🅰 🚲 **DRY** 🚗 👣 ★★★★ All
rooms en-suite

POSTCOMBE

 **SU7099** 🥾 **1.6 miles (2.5km)**
🚆 **Princes Risborough 8 miles (13km)**

S M T W T F S   S M T W T F S

🧺 |||||||||||
S M T W T F S

Pub: England's Rose 01844 281383

England's Rose | *Closed 25&26 Dec* | **INN** ▲

Ms Sheila Guinnane
London Road, Postcombe, Thame OX9 7AS
T: 01844 281383
E: info@englandsrosepub.co.uk
www.englandsrosepub.co.uk
🛏 3 £70 (£45) 🛏 4 £70 🛏 1
£45 ⚥ 🔲 V 🅰 🚲 **DRY** 🔲 🚗
👣 **VISA** Most major cards. All rooms
en-suite
▮ Camping by arrangement £8/person

ASTON ROWANT

 **SU7298** 🥾 **0.6 miles (1km)**
🚆 **Princes Risborough 6 miles (10km)**

S M T W T F S   S M T W T F S

Pub: Lambert Arms 01844 351496

☆ Aston Rowant National Nature
Reserve
T: 01844 351833
www.naturalengland.org.uk

Lambert Arms

Mr Andrew Edwards
London Road, Aston Rowant OX49 5SB
T: 01844 351496
E: info.lambertarms@bespokehotels.
com
www.bespokehotels.com/hotel/pages/
lambertarms/home.htm
🛏 31 £89 🛏 7 £89 🛏 1 £99
🚶‍♀️ ⟳ ▧ V ♦ ● 🕊 ◐ 🔖 💳 Most
major cards. ★★★★ All rooms
en-suite
ℍ £10 charge for dogs. Free WiFi

B&B **Tower Cottage** *closed Xmas & New Year*

Mrs Margaret Mason
Chinnor Road, Aston Rowant
OX49 5SH
T: 01844 354676
E: towercottagebb@aol.com
www.tower-cottage.co.uk
🛏 1 £55 🛏 2 £50 (£40) 🚶‍♀️ (min
age 4) V 🕊 🚲 **DRY** 🔄 🔖 📶 Some
rooms en-suite, one with private
bathroom

Spindle

STOKENCHURCH

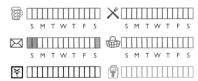

SU7696 🥾 **2.7 miles (4.3km)**
🚂 **Princes Risborough or High
Wycombe 7.3 miles (11.7km)**

£ Lloyds TSB & three 🖳 in local stores

Hallbottom Farm   B&B

Mrs Deborah Abbot
Park Lane, Stokenchurch HP14 3TQ
T: 01494 482520 **M:** 07778 216024
E: deborah@hallbottomfarm.co.uk
www.hallbottomfarm.co.uk
🛏 4 £80 🛏 2 £80 (£50) 🛏 1
£120 🚶‍♀️ ⟳ V ⓘ O 🚲 **DRY** 🔖 Some
rooms en-suite
ℍ Charge for lift to/from Ridgeway.
Free transport to evening meal

KINGSTON BLOUNT

SU7399 🥾 **0.5 miles (0.8km)**
🚂 **Princes Risborough 6 miles
(10km)**

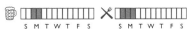

Pub: Cherry Tree 01844 355966

SC | **Lakeside Town Farm**

Mrs Theresa Clark
Town Farm Cottage, Brook Street,
Kingston Blount OX39 4RZ
T: 01844 352152 **M:** 07971 436504
E: theresa@townfarmcottage.co.uk
www.townfarmcottage.co.uk
VISA Most major cards
Self-catering facilities from £70 per
night, min stay 2 nights

INN | **Cherry Tree**

Mrs Kate Louise Hutton
High Street, Kingston Blount OX39 4SJ
T: 01844 355966 **M:** 07590 397753
E: info@cherrytreekingstonblount.co.uk
www.cherrytreekingstonblount.co.uk
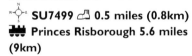 3 £60 1 £60
 All major
cards ★★★ All rooms en-suite
No evening meals Sundays &
Mondays

CROWELL

 SU7499 0.5 miles (0.8km)
**Princes Risborough 5.6 miles
(9km)**

S M T W T F S   S M T W T F S

Pub: Shepherd's Crook 01844 355266

CHINNOR

 SP7500 0.6 miles (1km)
**Princes Risborough 4 miles
(7km) P F** WC (closed Sat
afternoon and Sunday)
Large village with range of services

☆ Chinnor Hill Nature Reserve
T: 01865 775476 www.bbowt.org.uk

☆ Chinnor and Princes Risborough
Railway
T: 01844 353535
www.chinnorrailway.co.uk

SYDENHAM

 SP7301 2.2 miles (3.6km)
**Haddenham & Thame
Parkway 6.1 miles (9.8km)**

S M T W T F S   S M T W T F S

Pubs: Crown Inn 01844 351634 &
Inn at Emmington 01844 351367

Inn at Emmington | **INN**

Mr Jeremy Pattison
Sydenham Road, Sydenham, Chinnor
OX39 4LD
T: 01844 351367
E: theinnemmington@btconnect.com
www.theinnatemmington.co.uk
 7 £79 1 £89 (£70)
Most major
cards. All rooms en-suite
Additional charge for 3rd/4th person
in family room. No evening meal on
Sundays **79**

HENTON

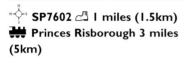 **SP7602** 🥾 I miles (1.5km)
🚂 **Princes Risborough 3 miles (5km)**

S M T W T F S   S M T W T F S

Pub: Peacock 01844 353519

B&B Manor Farm Cottage

Mr & Mrs Trevor & Jean Dixon
Henton, Chinnor OX39 4AE
T: 01844 353301 **M:** 07717 120000
E: dixonhenton@aol.com
www.manorfarmcottage.info
🛏 2 £64 (£48) 👫 🖪 V 🍎 O 🔥
🚲 **DRY** 🔲 👣 ★★★★ One room
en-suite, one private bathroom
🅷 VisitEngland Silver Award

Ⓗ Peacock   *closed Xmas Day*

Mr Martin Roberts
Henton, Chinnor OX39 4AH
T: 01844 353519
E: escape@peacockcountryinn.co.uk
www.peacockcountryinn.co.uk
🛏 18 £120 🥾 7 £120 (£110) 👫 ♿
🖪 V 🍎 O 🔥 🌀 🚲 🚗 👣 🛜 📶
All major cards. All rooms en-suite
🅷 Children under 8 free. Discounts
Fridays and Sundays

BLEDLOW

 **SP7702** 🥾 0.6 miles (1km)
🚂 **Princes Risborough 2 miles (3km)**

S M T W T F S   S M T W T F S

Pub: Lions of Bledlow 01844 343345

☆ Lyde Gardens (next to church) open
daily dawn to dusk.

SAUNDERTON LEE

 **SP7901** 🥾 0.6 miles (1km)
🚂 **Saunderton 1.2 miles (2km)**

S M T W T F S   S M T W T F S

Pubs: The Chiltern Hotel and
Restaurant 01844 345299
The Golden Cross 01494 565974

Chiltern Hotel and Restaurant 🏨

Scott Sandele
Wycombe Road, Saunderton, Princes
Risborough HP27 9NP
T: 01844 345299
E: info@the-chiltern.co.uk
www. the-chiltern.co.uk
🛏 9 £70 🥾 1 £90 🥾 1 £90 🛏 2
£60 👫 🖪 V 🍎 🌀 🛜 📶 All major
cards. All rooms en-suite

PRINCES RISBOROUGH

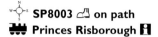 **SP8003** on path
Princes Risborough

Town with full range of services, visit www.visitchilterns.co.uk for further details. Farmers Market 3rd Thurs of each month.

B&B | **Ridgeway Lodge**

Mrs Miv Hughes
Upper Icknield Way, Saunderton, Princes Risborough HP27 9NL
T: 01844 345438 **M:** 07828 078848
E: miv@ridgewaylodge.co.uk
www.ridgewaylodge.co.uk
2 £90 2 £90 (£49) Some rooms en-suite.

WHITELEAF

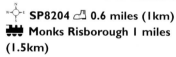 **SP8204** 0.6 miles (1km)
Monks Risborough 1 miles (1.5km)

S M T W T F S   S M T W T F S

Pub: Red Lion 01844 344476. Pub closes at 7pm during winter months on Sundays

☆ Whiteleaf Hill and Cross

| **Red Lion** | |

Anthony Hibbert
Upper Icknield Way, Whiteleaf, Princes Risborough HP27 0LL
T: 01844 344476 **M:** 07881 777240
E: tim_hibbert@hotmail.com
www.theredlionwhiteleaf.co.uk
2 £60 2 £60 Most major cards. All rooms en-suite
No evening meal Sundays and Mondays.

LOWER CADSDEN

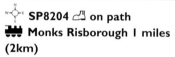 **SP8204** on path
Monks Risborough 1 miles (2km)

S M T W T F S   S M T W T F S

Pub: Plough at Cadsden 01844 343302

☆ Grangelands and Pulpit Hill Nature Reserve

| **Plough at Cadsden** | |

Mr Steve Hollings
Cadsden, Princes Risborough HP27 0NB
T: 01844 343302
E: info@plough-at-cadsden.co.uk
www.plough-at-cadsden.co.uk
1 £95 1 £110 1 £110 (£65)
1 £65 Most major cards. All rooms en-suite

ASKETT

✧ SP8105 🥾 1.2 miles (2km)
🚂 Monks Risborough 0.5 miles (1km)

B&B | **Solis Ortu**

Mrs Pamela Crockett
Aylesbury Road, Askett, Princes
Risborough HP27 9LY
T: 01844 347777 **M:** 07711 600540
E: p.and.pr@btinternet.com
🛏 1 £70 🛏 1 £70 (£35) 👫 (min
age 5) **V** 🚶 🚲 🚗 Double room
en-suite
🅷 Internet access

GREAT KIMBLE

✧ SP8206 🥾 0.6 miles (1km)
🚂 Little Kimble 0.5 miles (1km)

Pub: Swan 01844 275288

INN | **Swan at Great Kimble**

Mick Caffrey
Grove Lane, Great Kimble, Aylesbury
HP17 9TR
T: 01844 275288
E: kimbleswan@gmail.com
www.kimbleswan.co.uk
🛏 2 £60 🛏 1 £70 🛏 1 £70 👫 🏠
V 🍎 🚶 🐕 **DRY** 🅾 🚗 🐾 **VISA** Most
major cards. All rooms en-suite

BUTLERS CROSS

✧ SP8407 🥾 0.6 miles (1km)
🚂 Little Kimble 1 miles (2km)

Pub: Russell Arms 01296 624411

☆ Chiltern Brewery
T: 01296 613647
www.chilternbrewery.co.uk

WESTON TURVILLE

✧ SP8510 🥾 1.8 miles (2.9 km)
🚂 Stoke Mandeville 1.9 miles
(3km) **P F**

Pubs: Five Bells 01296 613131 &
Chandos Arms 01296 613532
Regular bus service from Wendover

INN | **Five Bells** | **INN**

Mr Nathan Mitchelson
40 Main Street, Weston Turville HP22
5RW
T: 01296 613131
E: info@innkeeperslodge.com
www.innkeeperslodge.com
🛏 9 £49 🛏 2 £49 🛏 5 £49 👫 **V**
🚫 📶 **VISA** All major cards. All rooms
en-suite
🅷 Continental breakfast

B&B | **Hamlet** | *closed 25 & 26 Dec*

Mr Mark Burgess
3 Home Close, Weston Turville
HP22 5SP
T: 01296 612660 **M:** 07840 335458
E: info@thehamletbandb.co.uk
www.thehamletbandb.co.uk
🛏 2 £60 🛏 1 £60 (£40) 🛏 1 £30
🕇🕇 (min age 4) 🚲 Some rooms
ensuite

WENDOVER

🧭 **SP8607** 🛌 **on path**
🚂 **Wendover** 🚻

Town with full range of services, visit
www.wendover-pc.gov.uk for further
details. Local Produce Market 3rd Sat of
each month 09.00-1:00pm.

☆ Wendover Woods
T: 01296 625825 www.forestry.gov.uk

B&B | **Mayertorne Cottage** | *closed Xmas*

2.5 miles(4km) south of Wendover

Mr Anthony Sykes
London Road, Wendover Dean HP22
6QA
T: 01296 620830
E: anthonysykes@btconnect.com
www.mayertorne.co.uk
🛏 1 £75 🛏 1 £75 (£70) 🕇🕇 📷 V
🍴 O 🏔 🚭 🚲 DRY 📺 🚶 🛜 One
room ensuite
🍲 £ by negotiation

Red Lion | 🏨

Mr Sam Hughes
High Street HP22 6DU
T: 01296 622266
E: redlionhotel.wendover@fullers.co.uk
www.redlionhotelwendover.co.uk
🛏 16 £89 🛏 3 £89 🛏 2 £99
🛏 2 £79 🕇🕇 ♿ V 🏔 🚭 🚲 🛜 VISA
All major cards. All rooms en-suite

17 Icknield Close | *closed Xmas* | **B&B**

Mrs G Samuels
Wendover HP22 6HG
T: 01296 583285
E: grbr.samuels@ntlworld.com
🛏 2 £70 🛏 1 £35 🕇🕇(min age 7) V 🍴
O 🚲 DRY 🛜 ★★★

17 Orchard Close | **B&B**

Mrs Thalia Lansdowne
Wendover HP22 6LN
T: 01296 623624
E: thalialansdowne@btopenworld.com
🛏 1 £55 (£45) 🏔 🚲 🛜
🚻 Continental breakfast

Wendover Woods

Bacombe Hill near Wendover

Whiteleaf

Section 6

Wendover to Ivinghoe Beacon

This 11.8 miles (18.8km) section is the most wooded of
The Ridgeway with extensive woods, many of beech, much of the
way. However once the Trail reaches Pitstone Hill the final few miles
are in open downland countryside reminiscent of the landscape
surrounding earlier stages. As a final flourish The Ridgeway finishes
on top of yet another Iron Age fort at Ivinghoe Beacon.

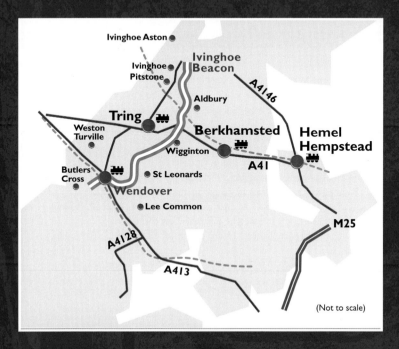

(Not to scale)

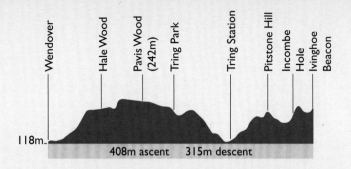

Wendover | Hale Wood | Pavis Wood (242m) | Tring Park | Tring Station | Pitstone Hill | Incombe Hole | Ivinghoe Beacon

118m

408m ascent   315m descent

Maps

| Landranger maps | 165 | Aylesbury and Leighton Buzzard |
| Explorer maps | 181 | Chiltern Hills North |

Taxis

Place	Name	Telephone Number
Wendover	Alexander's	01296 620888
Tring	Airport Taxis of Tring	01442 828848
	Aky Cars of Tring	07958 316063
	DMG Bev's of Tring	01442 824105
	John Taxi's	01442 828828
	Mark's Taxis	01442 824105
	Mike's Private Hire	01442 826161

Car Parking

If you choose to park in villages close to The Ridgeway, please park considerately. Other places to park are listed below but you need to be aware that theft from cars parked in the countryside does occur. You are advised to leave any unnecessary items at home or, failing that, ensure that anything valuable is locked in the boot of your vehicle.

Place	Map Grid Reference
Wendover public car park	SP 868077
Pitstone Hill car park east of Tring. From sharp bend on B488, ½ mile (1km) southeast of Ivinghoe, take minor road signposted Aldbury. Car park is on right after ½ mile (1km)	SP 955149
National Trust car park for Ivinghoe Beacon, on the left of minor road to Ringshall, ½ mile (1km) south off the B489	SP 962162

Toilets

Place	Map Grid Reference
Wendover (Library Car Park)	SP 868078

Vets

Place	Name	Telephone Number
Aylesbury	Hampden Veterinary Hospital*	01296 423666
	For equine	01296 745374
*Covers Watlington, Whiteleaf & Princes Risborough		
Halton	Wendover Heights Veterinary Centre	01296 623439
Tring	Springwell Veterinary Surgery	01442 822151

Horsebox Parking

The following place has sufficient space for you to park your horsebox. You **must** call in advance to arrange as space may be scarce. A fee may also be charged.

Place	Name	Telephone Number
Tring	Chivery Dairy (Accommodation guests)	01296 623065

Visitor Information Centres

These VICs are staffed but note that many libraries in the area also have leaflets about local attractions and events.

★ offers accommodation booking service (until 15:30)

Place	Address/Opening Hours
★Wendover	The Clock Tower, High Street, Wendover HP22 6DU
	T: 01296 696759 **E**: tourism@wendover-pc.gov.uk
	www.wendover-pc.gov.uk
	Opening hours: All year: Mon, Thur, Fri & Sat 10:00-16:00
Tring	99 Akeman Street, Tring HP23 6AA
	T: 01442 823347 **E**: info@tring.gov.uk
	www.tring.gov.uk
	Opening hours:
	All year: Mon-Sat 09:30-15:00, Sat 10:00-13:00

LEE COMMON

 SP9004 **1.9 miles (3km)**
Wendover 4.5 miles (7.3km)

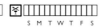
S M T W T F S   S M T W T F S

Pub: Cock and Rabbit/Graziemille
01494 837540

SC Lower Bassibones Farm

Mrs Anthea Hartley
Lee Common, Great Missenden
HP16 9LA
T: 01494 837798
E: lowerbassibones@yahoo.co.uk
www.discover-real-england.com
Most major cards
Self-catering accommodation
available at £295/week

ST LEONARDS

 SP8510 **2.5 miles (4 km)**
**Stoke Mandeville 1.9 miles
(3km) P F**

S M T W T F S   S M T W T F S

Pub: White Lion 01494 758387

WIGGINTON

 SP9310 **on path**
Tring 1 miles (2km)

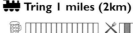
S M T W T F S   S M T W T F S

Pub: Greyhound Inn 01442 824631

☆ Tring Park
www.woodlandtrust.org.uk

Greyhound Inn - Wigginton

Natalie Batchelor
Chesham Road, Wigginton HP23 6EH
T: 01442 824631
E: thegreyhoundwigginton@hotmail.
co.uk
www.greyhoundtring.co.uk
1 £65 1 £65 (£50) 1 £80
Most
major cards. All rooms en-suite
No evening meal Sundays.

TRING

 SP9211 **1.2 miles (2km)**
Tring P£

Town with full range of services, visit
www.tring.gov.uk for further details.

☆ The Natural History Museum Tring
T: 0207 9426171 www.nhm.ac.uk/tring

☆ Grand Union Canal
www.canalrivertrust.org.uk

Ⓗ Pendley Manor Hotel

Mrs Claire Lee
Cow Lane, Tring HP23 5QY
T: 01442 891891
E: reception@pendley-manor.co.uk
www.pendley-manor.co.uk
🛏 54 £90 🛏 15 £100 🛏 2 £100
🛏 1 £80 ⁂ ♿ V 🍎 O Ⓞ 📶 VISA
All major cards ★★★★ All rooms
en-suite

Ⓗ Premier Inn

The Manager
Tring Hill, Tring HP23 4LD
T: 01442 824819/08715 279104
www.premierinn.com
🛏 30 £29 ⁂ ♿ 🔲 VISA All major
cards. All rooms en-suite
Ⓜ Prices are for room only. Restaurant
serving breakfast and evening meal
located on site

Chivery Dairy   B&B
⌖ SP901084 410m from Ridgeway   ◡

Ms Suzanne Myers
The Barns, Chivery Hall Farm, Tring
HP23 6LD
T: 01296 623065 **M:** 07881 628915
E: chiveryspa@yahoo.co.uk
🛏 1 £80 ⁂ ♿ 📷 🍴 O 🏍 Ⓞ 🚲
DRY 🔲
🐕 3 £10/night
Ⓜ Horsebox parking for accommodation
guests

Old Forge   B&B
Jane Bishop
54 High Street, Tring HP23 5AG
T: 01442 827038
E: theoldforgetring@btinternet.com
🛏 / 🛏 2 £80/£95 (£60) ⁂ V 🚲
DRY 🔲 All rooms en-suite
Ⓜ Continental breakfast

Ivinghoe Beacon

ALDBURY

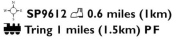 **SP9612** 👢 **0.6 miles (1km)**
🚂 **Tring 1 miles (1.5km) P F**

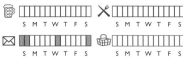

🅿 In village shop
Pubs: Greyhound 01442 851228 &
Valiant Trooper 01442 851203

☆ Aldbury Nowers Nature Reserve
www.hertswildlifetrust.org.uk

☆ Ashridge Estate
T: 01442 851227
www.nationaltrust.org.uk

B&B **Folly Farm**

Jude Glenister
Northfield Road, Aldbury HP23 5QJ
T: 01442 851645 **M:** 07775 847989
E: info@follyfarmbedandbreakfast.co.uk
www.follyfarmbedandbreakfast.co.uk
🛏 2 £75 (£70) 🛏 1 £50 **⚥** 🐱 **V** ☕
🐾 **DRY** 🚗 📶 Some rooms en-suite
🛁 Private bathroom. Lift to pub for
evening meal by arrangement

Greyhound Inn - Aldbury �INN

Mr Tim O'Gorman
19 Stocks Road, Aldbury HP23 5RT
T: 01442 851228
E: greyhound@aldbury.wanadoo.co.uk
www.greyhoundaldbury.co.uk
🛏 8 £75 🛏 2 £75 🛏 1 £90 (£65)
🛏 8 £65 **⚥ V** 🍎 **O** 🐾 **◐** 🚲 🚗
📶 **VISA** Most major cards. All rooms
en-suite

PITSTONE

 SP9315 👢 **1.6 miles (2.5km)**
🚂 **Tring 2 miles (4km) P F**

🅿 In general store
☆ Pitstone Windmill
T: 01442 851227
www.nationaltrust.org.uk

☆ Pitstone Green Museum
T: 01582 792701/01582 605464
www.pitstonemuseum.co.uk

Silver Birch Campsite   *closed* ⛺
                             1 Nov-Easter

⚡ SP947153 0.6miles(1km) from
Ridgeway

Mr S Newman
Upper Icknield Way, Pitstone, Leighton
Buzzard LU7 9EN
T: 01296 668348
⛺10 £8 **⚥** 📱 🔥 ♿

IVINGHOE

SP9416 0.9 miles (1.5km)
Tring 3 miles (5km)

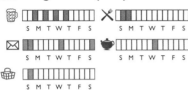

In post office.
Pubs: Rose & Crown 01296 668472
King's Head 01296 668388
Café: Sat & Sun 10:00-15:00

☆ Ford End Water Mill
T: 01442 825 421
www.fordendwatermill.co.uk

B&B Brownlow

SP934175 1.2 miles (1.9km)
northwest of Ivinghoe

Mrs Susan Kettler
Ivinghoe LU7 9DY
T: 01296 668787
E: info@thebrownlow.com
www.thebrownlow.com
3 £78 2 £78 1 £78 (£50)
(min age 6) V O DRY
Most major cards ★★★★ All rooms
en-suite
AA Gold Four Star Award. Lifts by
arrangement

Town Farm

SP950164 600m east of Ivinghoe
Mrs Leach
Ivinghoe, Leighton Buzzard LU7 9EL
T: 01296 668455
E: cwleach33@yahoo.co.uk
www.townfarmcamping.co.uk
20 £10/person 10 £20
WC DRY All
major cards
Children 0-3 free, 4-16 £5/person

IVINGHOE ASTON

SP9518 1 mile (1.5 km)
Stoke Tring 4.7 miles (7.56km)

Pub: The Village Swan 01525 220544.
Afternoon teas available 12:00-15:00
Tues-Sat

Laurel Cottage *closed Nov-Feb* SC

SP954180 1660m east of Ivinghoe
Mrs Jean Rayiru
Laurel Cottage, Ivinghoe Aston LU7 9DF
T: 01525 221548
E: laurelcs@aol.com
Self catering accommodation £35/night
10 £13

Ridgeway west just past Blowingstone

Upham bluebells

View from Wixen Bush

Coombe Hill

Distances between places along the The Ridgeway in miles

	Overton Hill	Ogbourne St George	Fox Hill	Uffington Castle	Sparsholt Firs	A338 (Wantage)	Bury Down	Streatley	Mongewell Park	Nuffield	Watlington	Chinnor	Princes Risborough	Wendover	Wigginton
Ogbourne St George	9.3														
Fox Hill	17.0	7.7													
Uffington Castle	22.3	13.0	5.3												
Sparsholt Firs	25.3	16.0	8.3	3.0											
A338 (Wantage)	29.1	19.8	12.1	6.8	3.8										
Bury Down	34.5	25.2	17.5	12.2	9.2	5.4									
Streatley	42.7	33.4	25.7	20.4	17.4	13.6	8.2								
Mongewell Park	48.5	39.2	31.5	26.2	23.2	19.4	14.0	5.8							
Nuffield	52.4	43.1	35.4	30.1	27.1	23.3	17.9	9.7	3.9						
Watlington	58.0	48.7	41.0	35.7	32.7	28.9	23.5	15.3	9.5	5.6					
Chinnor	63.7	54.4	46.7	41.4	38.4	34.6	29.2	21.0	15.2	11.3	5.7				
Princes Risborough	68.5	59.2	51.5	46.2	43.2	39.4	34.0	25.8	20.0	16.1	10.5	4.8			
Wendover	75.0	65.7	58.0	52.7	49.7	45.9	40.5	32.3	26.5	22.6	17.0	11.3	6.5		
Wigginton	81.5	72.2	64.5	59.2	56.2	52.4	47.0	38.8	33.0	29.1	23.5	17.8	13.0	6.5	
Ivinghoe Beacon	86.8	77.5	69.8	64.5	61.5	57.7	52.3	44.1	38.3	34.4	28.8	23.1	18.3	11.8	5.3